Paul Auster

Moon Palace

von Karl Erhard Schuhmacher

Klett Lernen und Wissen

Karl Erhard Schuhmacher, Gymnasiallehrer für Englisch, Geschichte und Sozialkunde in Rheinland-Pfalz; Fachleiter für Englisch.

Beratende Mitarbeit: Harald Weisshaar

Paul Austers Roman *Moon Palace* liegt als Klettbuch unter ISBN 978-3-12-573835-5 (Stuttgart: Ernst Klett Sprachen, 2007) vor. Auf diese Ausgabe beziehen sich die Seitenangaben der Lektürehilfe.

Bibliographische Information Der Deutschen Bibliothek
Die Deutsche Bibliothek verzeichnet diese Publikation in der Deutschen Nationalbibliographie; detaillierte bibliographische Daten sind im Internet über http://dnb.ddb.de abrufbar

Auflage 5. 4. 3. 2. 1. | 2012 2011 2010 2009 2008
Die letzten Zahlen bezeichnen jeweils die Auflage und das Jahr des Druckes.

Umschlagfoto: Corbis, Düsseldorf/Deborah Feingold
Satz: DOPPELPUNKT Auch & Grätzbach GbR, Stuttgart
Druck: Druck Partner Rübelmann, Hemsbach
Printed in Germany
ISBN: 978-3-12-923046-6

9 783129 230466

Contents

The Author and his Times

The Author's Life and Works

Paul Auster was born in Newark (New Jersey) on February 3, 1947, as a descendant of Jewish immigrants from Austria. He grew up in the Newark suburbs of South Orange and Maplewood (New Jersey), which is only 20 miles southwest of New York. He attended high school in Maplewood.

> "I came from a middle-class family. My childhood was comfortable, and I never suffered from any wants and deprivations that plague most of the human beings who live on this earth. I never went hungry, I never was cold, I never felt in danger of losing the things I had." (Paul Auster, *Hand to Mouth*, p. 6)

This fairly positive view of his childhood seems to refer to the material side of his life only. His father Samuel Auster was a businessman. As a landlord, he had to look after his houses and see that rent money came in. He was therefore often absent from home. He would leave early in the morning without having seen his boy and return home when Paul was already in bed. As a boy, Paul Auster suffered much from his father's remoteness and his unwillingness to engage in a close relationship. In contrast to this, his mother, Queenie Auster, gave him extra love and much attention, the more so as the boy did not enjoy good health.

> "I was my mother's boy, and I lived in her orbit. I was a little moon circling her gigantic earth. [...] We spent a lot of time together, she in her loneliness and I in my cramps, waiting patiently in doctor's offices [...] I would cling to these doctors in a desperate sort of way, wanting them to hold me. From the very beginning, it seems, I was looking for my father, looking frantically for anyone who resembled him." (Paul Auster, *The Invention of Solitude*, pp. 20–21)

Paul became very fond of reading, although his parents were not particularly interested in it. An uncle of his, Allan Mandelbaum, stored several boxes of books at the Austers' home while he went away on a longer trip to Europe. Paul Auster, still in his early teens at that time, read one book after the other and developed a great love for books and reading. At high school one of Auster's favorite activities was sports. He liked playing basketball and he was an extremely enthusiastic baseball player. He was the star of his team, which played in the "Little League". His father came just once to watch a match, but then, of course, Paul played very badly. His father's reaction was indifferent and revealed to Paul that his father had no real interest in him. "Whether I succeeded or failed did not essentially matter to him." (Paul Auster, *The Invention of Solitude,* p. 24)

At the age of 8, Paul was taken to a home match of the New York Giants, his favorite team, probably by his grandfather who was a great baseball fan. At that time, the New York Giants, a team which no longer exists, had a great star called Will Mays, who was Paul's idol. So Paul was, of course, very excited to finally see him play. When Paul even happened to meet Will Mays after the match, he screwed up all his courage and went up to him to ask him for an autograph. As neither he nor Will Mays had a pencil on them, Mays said: "Sorry, kid. Ain't got no pencil, can't give no autograph." From that day on it became Auster's habit never to leave the house without a pencil.

> "If nothing else, the years have taught me this: if there is a pencil in your pocket, there's a good chance that one day you'll feel tempted to start using it. As I like to tell my children, that's how I became a writer." (Paul Auster, "Why Write?", in: *The New Yorker,* December 25, 1995)

In another interview, however, Auster gave the more probable explanation that, at the age of 15, he was so fascinated by Dostoyevsky's *Crime and Punishment* that he decided to become a writer.

> "All along, my only ambition had been to write. I had known that as early as sixteen or seventeen years old, and I had never deluded myself into thinking I could make a living at it. Becoming a writer is not a 'career decision' like becoming a doctor or a policeman. You don't choose so much as get chosen, and once you accept the fact that you're not fit for anything else, you have to be prepared to walk a long, hard road for the rest of your days. [...] All I wanted was a chance to do the work I felt I had it in me to do." (Paul Auster, *Hand to Mouth,* pp. 3–4)

In his last high school year, Paul Auster's parents got divorced. Paul and his sister moved to an apartment with their mother while his father stayed alone in the large family house. His mother married again and Paul Auster developed a good relationship to his stepfather, who time and again helped him out in critical situations. After high school graduation (1966), he took all his savings, money from odd jobs, and money given to him by relatives, to spend two and a half months in Europe. He stayed in Paris for a month and then traveled to Italy, Spain and to Ireland. He spent all his money and lived on almost nothing for some time to arrive home having lost more than twenty pounds in weight.

In 1966, he enrolled at Columbia University (New York City) where he studied English and Comparative Literature. The late 1960s were the times of the student revolt. The students protested against the Vietnam War and asked for democratic participation at universities. In 1968, unrest and riots at Columbia University led to its temporary shutdown.

> "I took part in some things and kept my distance from others. I helped occupy one of the campus buildings, was roughed up by cops and spent a night in jail, but mostly I was a by-stander, a sympathetic fellow traveller." (Paul Auster, *Hand to Mouth*, p. 34)

During his university years, he wrote a fair amount of poems, started two novels – but did not complete them –, wrote several plays, translated French poetry into English and published articles on books and films in the *Columbia Daily Spectator*. Having received his B.A. (1969) and M.A. (1970) degrees in English and Comparative Literature, Auster left Columbia University. Instead of pursuing a career, he first went to sea for a year as an ordinary seaman on an oil tanker in the Gulf of Mexico. In spite of his father's wish for him to become a businessman, Paul took the money he had earned at sea to move to France (1971). He stayed there for four years – most of the time in Paris. He had various jobs, but hardly scraped together a living. First he lived on his savings and when those ran out he lived on the money he earned in various jobs as a tutor, a translator of art books, a telephone operator and an assistant to a film producer. For some time he had barely enough money to survive – the "art of hunger" was a daily experience to him. He began translating the works of French writers into English and published some of his own poems and essays. He also met the famous dramatist Samuel Beckett, who left a lasting impression on him.

When after four years Auster returned to New York, he worked as a translator of French writers and started to teach literature at Columbia University. In 1974, he published his first volume of poetry (*Unearth*), but it did not meet with much success. In the late seventies, Auster went through a critical period. He was hardly able to make a living. His marriage to Lydia Davis – his companion in France – with whom he has a son, ended in divorce (1978). Additionally, his creative powers had somehow run dry. In 1980, Paul Auster's father died on the morning he had finished writing the essay *White Spaces*, a literary response to a dance performance which had left a deep impression on him. Auster saw this coincidence as a compelling occurrence. Being alone and living on the modest inheritance from his father, Paul Auster felt driven to write a book about his father to come to terms with this difficult man and his unhappy relationship to him. *The Invention of Solitude* was published in 1982 and especially its first part (*Portrait of an Invisible Man*) was regarded as a literary success. *The Art of Hunger,* a collection of essays and interviews, also appeared in 1982. The title piece is a comparison of Knut Hamsun's novel *Hunger* and Kafka's story *A Hunger Artist.*

> "In each, the protagonist willingly starves himself in what is at once an artistic act in itself and a way of confronting life – and death – with no support systems." (Judith Graham, ed., *Current Biography Yearbook 1996,* p. 13)

Auster had had ideas for novels while he was still at college; but only now, after these first successes, did he undertake serious attempts at giving full form to them. The first results of his fiction writing were three detective stories, *City of Glass, Ghosts* and *The Locked Room,* which were published between 1985 and 1987. These three novellas were soon published in the form of one book with the title *The New York Trilogy* (1987) which became a great success. It found enthusiastic readers in both America and Europe.
Within the next few years, Paul Auster turned out to be a very prolific writer. He wrote and published five great novels which established him as a major contemporary American novelist: *In the Country of Last Things* (1987), *Moon Palace* (1989), *The Music of Chance* (1990), *Leviathan* (1992), *Mr. Vertigo* (1994). His work has been translated into more than 20 languages.
In the 1990s, Paul Auster turned his attention to film making. He wrote the screenplay for the internationally successful *Smoke* (1995). It depicts life in his home borough of Brooklyn. In cooperation with Wayne Wang, he produced and directed *Blue in the Face* (1995). *Lulu on the Bridge* (1998) was the first film Auster directed on his own. He also published his memoirs *Hand to Mouth* (1997) and the novel *Timbuktu* (1999), whose protagonist is a dog.
After the turn of the century Paul Auster has published four novels which were all well recieved by critics and the public. *The Book of Illusions* (2002) in which he presents a story circling around a lost film from the silent cinema was a national bestseller. To some it is Auster's richest, most emotionally charged novel so far. In 2006 he was awarded the prestigious Prince of Asturias prize for literature, thus joining Günter Grass, Doris Lessing and Arthur Miller.
Auster has been married to the writer Siri Hustvedt since 1981. They have a daughter, Sophie, and live in Brooklyn, New York City.

The Political Climate

Auster's protected childhood coincides with the relatively quiet after-war period of the late 1940s and 50s, the years in which Truman (1945–1953) and Eisenhower (1953–1961) were American presidents. The end of World War II gave a tremendous boost to the American economy. The middle classes grew and most Americans enjoyed greater material wealth. Household machines made life easier, and the car made virtually everyone mobile. All this was accompanied by a general feeling of optimism. In the late forties, the birth rate went up considerably, so that people began to speak of a baby boom. The generation of Paul Auster (*1947), Bill Clinton (*1947), Al Gore (*1948), George W. Bush Jr. (*1948) were and still are called the "baby boomers". The baby boomers as a specific generation have played a significant role in the social and economic development of the USA. For instance, as this generation entered its teens, it caused an enormous expansion in high school and college education in the 1950s and 1960s. The Cold War and the Berlin Air Lift (1948/49), and the involvement in the Korean War on the side of South Korea were expressions of the Truman Doctrine – a guideline for US foreign policy "to support free peoples who are resisting [...] outside pressures" (Truman). The Eisenhower years saw the beginning of desegregation in American society and the beginning of the struggle of black Americans for equal rights. The fight for civil rights began with the 1954 decision of the Supreme Court in the case Brown vs. Board of Education, which ruled that it was unconstitutional for US states to maintain separate schools for black and white children. The struggle against discrimination was led by Martin Luther King, whose non-violent Civil Rights Movement carried out many campaigns in the 1960s to create equal opportunities for blacks (1963 March on Washington; the fight for equality in education, housing and voting).

The Kennedy (1961–1963) and Johnson (1963–1969) administrations were years of great prosperity and unparalleled economic wealth. The American Way of Life was based on an abundance of resources and goods. The USA came to be known as the "affluent society" (*affluent* is another word for *rich*), a term coined by J. K. Galbraith in 1958. At the same time, there were many underprivileged people in the USA, some of whom lived in great poverty. In the Johnson years, the US government recognized its social responsibility to help these people with many programs which came to be known as the "War on Poverty". The so-called "Sputnik Shock", which refers to the shock the Soviet Union gave Americans by launching the first earth-orbiting vehicle and sending the first Cosmonaut – Yuri Gagarin – around the earth, sparked off

various specific programs to advance school and university education. Kennedy announced a program to land American astronauts on the moon before the Russians. The challenge of the space program was seen as the challenge of a "new frontier" and it was widely supported by the public despite its heavy cost. Thus, it was a day of national pride when in July 1969 live television showed Neil Armstrong's first step on the moon: "That's one small step for a man, one giant leap for mankind." (Neil Armstrong) Scientific advances (polio vaccine), new technologies and products (synthetic textiles, transistors, computers) were proof that the USA was finding the right answers to the technological challenges. Once more, America became very attractive to immigrants. A new wave of immigration followed the Immigration Act of 1965, which based immigration not so much on nationality, but on the skills and abilities of the newcomers. In this way, the longstanding ban on Chinese immigration was lifted after almost a whole century.
The mood of optimism, however, changed dramatically when the war in Vietnam (1964–1973) escalated. A general draft was enacted and more and more American soldiers were sent to Vietnam. Anti-war protests and riots at the 1968 Democratic convention were manifestations of a deeply divided nation: There were the "doves" who wanted to stop the war, and the "hawks" who wanted to continue and end the war successfully to prevent the spread of communist control in Vietnam and all Southeast Asia ("domino theory"). Students were exempted from the general draft. Despite having completed their studies, many found ways to get around the draft ("draft dodgers"). They started studies at foreign universities (Bill Clinton), went to Canada or entered the service of the National Guard (George W. Bush) at home. Because of a conflict with the French director of his Year Abroad Program, Auster left Paris and – in a rigorous and rash move – Columbia University as well.

> "It was a crazy thing to do. The prospect of not getting a B.A. didn't worry me, but turning my back on college meant that I would automatically lose my student deferment. With the troop buildup in Vietnam growing at an alarming rate, I had suddenly put myself in a good position to be drafted into the army. That would have been fine if I supported the war, but I didn't. I was against it, and nothing was ever going to make me fight in it. If they tried to induct me into the army, I would refuse to serve. If they arrested me, I would go to jail."
> (Paul Auster, *Hand to Mouth,* pp. 30–31)

As there were too many young men to be considered for the draft, Auster was given the chance to take part in a draft lottery which selected those who had to go. He was lucky: He drew a very high number that meant that he neither had to go to Vietnam nor to jail. Both in *Moon Palace* and in *Levia-*

than, Auster gives literary expression of his generation's critical attitude towards the war in Vietnam. The war ended in a defeat for the USA. President Nixon (1969–1974) continuously withdrew troops (from 500,000 in 1968 to 100,000 in 1972) and after heavy bombing on Hanoi a peace treaty was signed which concluded the American involvement in the war. Nearly 50,000 Americans had lost their lives, many had been wounded and came home traumatized.
The Watergate Affair (Nixon had allowed the Democratic Party to be illegally observed) forced Nixon to resign in 1974. The politically-minded generation of 68 gave way to the so-called "me-generation", made up of young people who were more interested in their personal economic success than in politics. The era of Ronald Reagan (1981–1989) restored national pride and a renewed belief in individualism and private entrepreneurship. Auster seems to have been on the side of people who saw this development less favorably. In *Leviathan* he characterizes the former 68er Sachs, who maintains his attitude of social criticism even in the Reagan era:

> "Sachs came to be seen as a throwback, as someone out of step with the spirit of the time. The world had changed around him, and in the present climate of selfishness and intolerance, of moronic, chest-pounding Americanism, his opinions sounded harsh and moralistic. It was bad enough that the (political) Right was everywhere in the ascendant, but even more disturbing to him was the collapse of any effective opposition to it. The Democratic Party had carved in; the left had all but disappeared; the press was mute." (*Leviathan*, pp. 116–117)

One hotly debated issue in these especially patriotic years was the question whether the burning of the US flag, the "Stars and Stripes", as a form of protest was a criminal offence. Auster comments on this in *Leviathan* and compares the national symbols of the Flag and the Statue of Liberty.

> "Unlike the flag, which tends to divide people as much as it brings them together, the statue is a symbol that causes no controversy. If many Americans are proud of their flag, there are many others who feel ashamed of it, and for every person who regards it as a holy object, there is another who would like to spit on it, or burn it, or drag it through the mud. The Statue of Liberty is immune from these conflicts. For the past hundred years, it has transcended politics and ideology, standing at the threshold of our country as an emblem of all that is good within us. It represents hope rather than reality, faith rather than facts, and one would be hard-pressed to find a single person willing to denounce the things it stands for: democracy, freedom, equality under the law. It is the best of what America has to offer the world, and however pained one might be by

> America's failure to live up to those ideals, the ideals themselves are not in question. They have given comfort to millions. They have instilled the hope in all of us that we might one day live in a better world." (*Leviathan*, p. 242)

Here, Auster, the descendant of Austrian immigrants, expresses his fundamental belief in America as a beacon of hope for all suppressed people in the world and as a country which has enabled generations of immigrants to fulfill their dreams. He is convinced of its democratic system, its open society and its fundamental values.

Influences on the Author's Works

Auster's writings often center on New York and especially Brooklyn. New York is seen as the vibrant city of the second half of the 20th century and the city of famous baseball teams. In his novels, he often features cosmopolitan Manhattan, Columbia University and Brooklyn with its pleasant residential areas and its museum, and quite often he discusses the ups and downs of various baseball teams and players. New York City is often compared to a labyrinth. The characters walk its streets to solve a puzzle. They try to get to know and understand the city, but never really get to grips with it.
Auster's works reveal a closeness to New England and its writers Emerson, Thoreau and Hawthorne, whom he studied at university and often mentions in his books. New England's cultural climate seems to attract Auster, as he regularly seeks retreat there.
With his academic background and his broad theoretical literary knowledge, Auster is well aware of the development of fiction in the second half of the 20th century from modernism to postmodernism. Elements of postmodernism can easily be detected in Auster's books: The fundamental doubts of whether language and texts can represent reality and express truth, the shifting perspectives within the novels, making use of various fictive narrators including the real author, the integration of books within books, the cross references between individual books. All these devices are used to deconstruct reality and are regarded as postmodern elements of fiction. With Auster's many specific and concrete references to place and time, one might read his novels as true stories. Many of the events are, however, so improbable, absurd and coincidental that his books clearly transcend reality.

The Plot

Moon Palace consists of three lines of action, which are interwoven in a complex way (see graph "Time Structure", pp. 48–49). These three lines circle around the three main characters of the novel: Marco Fogg, Solomon Barber and Thomas Effing. Gradually the novel brings to light that the three main characters are directly related to each other. Marco Fogg is Sol Barber's son who in turn is Effing's son. The absence of fathers is one of the novel's main themes.

The novel starts with a retrospect in which the narrator, Marco Fogg, briefly informs the reader about his childhood, his mother, his uncle and his school years. He is born in Boston and grows up with his mother, Emily Fogg, but without a father. Marco is not told by his mother who his father is, but finds an ideal foster father in his uncle. After his mother's death, Uncle Victor sees him through his school days, devising a financial scheme to assure that there is enough money to pay for a college education, too. Marco attends college at Columbia University. He first lives in the college dormitory, but then takes his own room which has a view of a Chinese restaurant and its large neonsign: MOON PALACE. When Uncle Victor, who is a clarinetist, goes on a longer tour with a band, he leaves his 1492 books to Marco. Marco takes them to his apartment and uses the boxes of books as furniture. When his substitute father suddenly dies, Marco is so profoundly affected that he falls into a deep crisis, losing contact to the world around him. He opens every box of Uncle Victor's books, and one by one he reads every book. In this way Marco somehow relives his uncle's intellectual life and incorporates his experiences into his own life.

Even his good friend and classmate Zimmer cannot help him to overcome his personal crisis. He withdraws from everybody and as his financial funds start to dwindle he lives a life of deprivation. In order to buy some food, he sells his uncle's books one by one at a second-hand bookshop. Nevertheless, he cannot avoid being turned out of his room so that one day he has to walk out into the streets of New York. He finds refuge in Central Park, where in the summer of 1969 it is not too hard to survive since there is enough leftover food from the many visitors. But in a spell of bad weather, Marco catches severe flu. He withdraws to a cave in Central Park. His health deteriorates, he suffers from hallucinations, and in the end he loses consciousness. But he is miraculously saved at the last minute by his friend Zimmer and the Chinese ballet student Kitty who Marco had met at Zimmer's old apartment. Zimmer puts Marco up and helps the extremely thin and weak dropout to recover and find courage again to go on with his life. Marco falls in love with Kitty and this fills him with new hope.

He finds employment as the companion of Thomas Effing, a rich old man in a wheelchair. He lives in Effing's house, reads books aloud to him and wheels him through the streets of New York. Soon Marco is given the task to write down Thomas Effing's life story, which is dictated to him by the blind man. Effing tells his story at great length; his narrative functions as a tale within the tale. Its significance for Marco's story is gradually opened up to the reader, and at the end of the novel we can establish the grandfather-father-son-line from Effing to Barber and Marco himself.

Thomas Effing, born Julian Barber, is the son of a rich industrialist. He becomes a landscape painter and marries a frigid wife whom he leaves for an expedition to the American West. On the last night before his departure to the West, Julian Barber fathers a son, Solomon Barber. Both never see each other, although Thomas Effing later on learns about his existence, but does not contact him. With his expedition to the West, Thomas Effing expects to experience the vastness of the American continent. As a painter, he hopes to achieve the emotional attitude towards Nature expressed in the landscape paintings of Blakelock and Thomas Moran. His expedition turns out to become a Wild West event. He is betrayed by his scout, is left back in the wilderness in Utah, and has to live in a cave for almost a year. He spends most of his time painting. One day, three notorious gunmen appear. Having been warned about them by an Indian, Effing is well-prepared and kills all three of them. He takes their money and horses and makes his way to California. Here he assumes a new identity and calls himself Thomas Effing. He becomes rich by investing the stolen money, but one day he is recognized as Julian Barber. He withdraws from society and leads a night life with dubious pleasures. One night, on his way home, he is mugged. He falls, slides along the street and crashes against a lamp-post, leaving his backbone broken. He sells all his possessions and goes to Paris. With his broken backbone he depends on help, and so he employs Pavel Shum as a companion. In the late 1930s, just before the Germans occupy Paris, Thomas Effing leaves France and returns to New York. After almost thirty years of service, Pavel Shum dies in a street accident, leaving his job to Marco Fogg. Marco Fogg is in Effing's service as a kind of secretary for half a year. He has the task of writing down Effing's story of his second life. Before Thomas Effing dies on May 12th, he instructs

Marco to get into contact with his son Solomon Barber to hand him over his inheritance and the "obituary" about his second life.
Marco dutifully does as he is told and contacts Solomon Barber. Solomon Barber is a history professor at a small Midwestern college, and to meet Marco he comes to New York for a few days. Marco is confronted with a colossal but very intelligent man. Solomon Barber, at the age of 63, is to hear the amazing story of his father's second life, whom he thought to have died a few months before his (Solomon's) birth. He is so intrigued by the account of Effing's Wild West experience that he wants to find the cave to check the truth of this story. He invites Marco to accompany him. Marco gladly agrees (as his love to Kitty has been destroyed by her decision to have an abortion) and joins Solomon on his trek to the West. They decide to go to Chicago first to visit the grave of Marco's mother. At this stage in the novel, the reader is aware of Solomon Barber's relationship to Marco's mother, but Marco is not: Solomon Barber, an excellent student and an outstanding historian, had taken his first teaching position at the provincial Oldham College (Ohio). Here he started an affair with a young student by the name of Emily Fogg. They were caught in the act, Emily Fogg fled home and Solomon Barber was dismissed. Emily became pregnant and gave birth to a boy she called Marco. She never told anyone, including Marco, about the identity of Marco's father.
Now that both are in Chicago, Solomon Barber and Marco Fogg visit Emily's grave. (Soon after his first meetings with Marco Fogg, Solomon Barber realized that this young man must be his son, but did not reveal the fact to Marco.) Standing at Emily's grave, Solomon Barber cannot suppress his feelings, and he has to admit to Marco that he was his mother's lover and that he is Marco's father. At this emotional moment, something highly improbable happens. Solomon Barber falls into an empty grave nearby and seriously hurts his back. He has to go to hospital, and two months later he dies. He leaves a confused Marco behind, who having just found his father has lost him again.
In great bewilderment about his new identity and in deep depression, Marco pursues the original plan and goes West. He finds that Effing's cave had been flooded two years before when a lake was created. At this place, Marco's car and money are stolen and so he starts walking westward on foot. He is prepared to walk to the end of the world in order to overcome his crisis.
During his long walk, his mood changes from fury and despair to a growing sense of happiness and peace of mind. After three months on foot, on January 6th 1972, he walks down to Laguna Beach in California to watch the moon rise over the Pacific.

The development of Marco's and Kitty's love for each other runs parallel to the stories of the male protagonists. This line of action, however, does not really determine the plot. They fall in love at first sight, but it takes long for them to declare their love for each other. Although Kitty saves Marco's life, it is Zimmer, who, with his material and psychological support, helps Marco to recover. Kitty keeps a reserved distance at that time. With the sudden and vehement outbreak of love after a chance meeting, the reader expects the love relationship to play a more dominant role in the novel. However, its development is only touched upon in passing, while Marco focuses his main interest on his life with Effing and Effing's life story. After Effing's death, the couple take a flat together and they settle down in happiness. The conflict about whether to have an abortion or not leads to the break-up of their relationship, a fact which allows Marco to set out for his journey to the West. It seems that the Kitty Wu episode is to a great extent only functional to the main lines of the plot. Kitty and Marco will not meet again.

The Story

Chapter I

Marco Stanley Fogg – his family, his college years, his crisis

The first two pages of the book are like an opening fanfare. In a very condensed way the narrator and protagonist presents the backbone of the whole story, although this is done so cleverly and in such a cryptic fashion that we don't realize the fact until we read the novel a second time. Marco Stanley Fogg presents details about himself, his family, his years at Columbia University (N.Y.) and his lapse into a deep personal crisis. He assumes a much later point of time, namely 1986 from which he looks back on his life in the late sixties. He begins his narrative with his freshman year at Columbia University in the autumn of 1965 when he is 18 years old. In a flashback (pp. 7–21), the narrator sums up his life leading up to his freshman year at Columbia.
Marco Fogg is born in 1947 as the only child of Emily Fogg, who does not marry his father and does not reveal his father's identity to Marco. Mother and son live in Boston together until Emily is killed in a road accident at the age of 29. So in February 1958, Marco, who is eleven years at that time, moves to his mother's brother in Chicago. Uncle Victor – a clarinetist – looks after little Marco very well. There is a close and warm relationship between uncle and nephew. They both share a great interest in baseball; they like to play all kinds of games together and they even invent some. "He knew that fatherhood was beyond him, and therefore he treated me less than as a child than as a friend." (p. 12) Soon after Marco's arrival, Uncle Victor takes him to the cinema to watch *Around the World in 80 Days* which is to have a great effect on Marco because the hero of Jule Verne's book and of the movie is called Phileas Fogg, his namesake. All the elements of Marco's name refer to traveling and make him a born traveller like Jule Verne's Phileas. Marco alludes to the medieval traveller Marco Polo, his middle name Stanley, refers to the American journalist Henry M. Stanley who tracked down Dr. Livingstone in the jungle, and Fogg itself – a wrong name given to his grandfather at Ellis Island during the immigration procedure – goes back to *Fogelman*, denoting a man who can fly like a bird.

Uncle Victor keeps stock of the compensation money from Emily's accident to pay for Marco's high school and college years. When Victor marries and the marriage turns out to be difficult, Marco Fogg – who is fifteen at that time – is sent to a boarding school in New Hampshire and spends three years there. Uncle Victor, who once played in the prestigious Cleveland Orchestra and had to leave it because he made a dirty joke within earshot of the concertmaster, first plays in a small combo called MOONLIGHT MOODS and then, after divorce from his wife, he founds a new group, the MOON MEN. When this group goes on a long tour to the American West in 1965, Uncle Victor dissolves his household and gives Marco his most valuable belongings: all his books – 1492 volumes –, a collection of baseball autographs and his tweed suit. Marco takes these things, including the many boxes filled with books, to New York when he starts college in 1965. After the first term at Columbia in which Marco is required to stay at the college dormitory, he moves to a private apartment on West 112th Street, fifth floor, to live alone there for the following three years. He furnishes the empty room with Victor's books, using the 76 boxes for chairs, table and bed. From his window he can look out through a gap between the houses down to Broadway to see the huge neon sign of a Chinese restaurant called MOON PALACE. In his first two college years, Marco assumes the pose of a sublime intellectual, a future genius, a man much more mature than his classmates. He reads avidly, shows off his literary knowledge, behaves like an eccentric, which is underlined by the fact that in the age of blue jeans he always wears Uncle Victor's tweed suit. According to the narrator, the student Marco Stanley Fogg gives the impression of being "gaunt, disheveled, intense, a young man clearly out of step with the rest of the world." (p. 22) Nevertheless, he seems to have friends, although he is not very specific about them; his closest and only real friend is his former roommate from the dormitory called David Zimmer. Besides the facts that Marco is over six feet tall and weighs 154 pounds (about 70 kg) – a tall and very slim young man – we know nothing else about his outer appearance.

Uncle Victor, who after the break-up of his Moon Men ends up as a door-to-door salesman for encyclopaedias in Idaho, suddenly dies from a heart attack in his flat in Boise. Marco is informed about this by a police officer called Neil Armstrong. Marco, who is twenty at that time, and one of Victor's friends arrange the funeral in Chicago, where Victor is buried beside Marco's mother. The loss of his uncle and foster father throws Marco off-course and into a deep personal crisis. At the same time, Marco becomes aware that his funds will be exhausted by the beginning of his senior (fourth) year as his expenses have been greater than expected. Alone his promise to Uncle Victor to graduate and the fear of being drafted into the army for service in Vietnam make him stay at Columbia. Marco, however, is not able to take any pragmatic action to improve his financial situation. In an act of general despair, accompanied by a deep disgust at the world and its upheavals, Marco decides not to do anything, to withdraw completely, to refuse himself to the world. He knows that this will lead to a "total eclipse", but "the image of that darkness gradually lured me in, seduced me with the simplicity of its design. […] The moon would block the sun, and at that point I would vanish." (p. 28) Marco Fogg seems to have fallen into a serious depression which is characterized by deep apathy and a longing for death. Two weeks after Victor's funeral, Marco begins reading his uncle's books. He does not work through the books with an academic mind. He regards the process of reading more as a way to come to terms with his uncle's death. It almost took the form of a reenactment of Victor's mental life.

> "Each time I opened a box, I was able to enter another segment of my uncle's life, a fixed period of days or weeks or months, and it consoled me to feel that I was occupying the same mental space that Victor once occupied – reading the same words, living in the same stories, perhaps thinking the same thoughts." (p. 29)

Due to his precarious financial situation, Marco is compelled to sell the books for little money at a second-hand bookstore. He finds the occasions at the second-hand bookshop extremely depressing, especially because its owner, Mr. Chandler, sees books only as objects whose value depends on their material quality alone. Forced by his increasing financial problems, Marco starts a process of divesting himself of all the amenities of modern life. He increasingly cuts down on expenses for food, living a life barely over subsistence level. He cancels his phone, his electricity is disconnected, he stops smoking and drinking and going out. As his books are sold to the second-hand store one by one, his 'furniture' vanishes as well till his room is virtually empty. He finally sells his typewriter and Uncle Victor's collection of autographs, but the little money he is paid for them does not carry him far. He hardly eats anything so that within three months he has lost considerable weight: from 154 pounds (about 70 kg) in June (1969) it goes down to 123 pounds (about 55 kg) in August (p. 37).

His mind begins to wander, he has hallucinations and loses his mental capacities. At the beginning of this deterioration, Marco gives Zimmer all kinds of eccentric explanations to avoid admitting that he has money problems.

They even lose contact when Zimmer changes his apartment. When Marco finally decides to ask Zimmer for help and tries to find him at his old address, he is greeted by a group of students throwing a house-warming party for one of their friends. He is invited to take part in their breakfast feast and hungrily wolfs down a lot of food, playing the eccentric fool in the company. One of the guests is the Chinese girl Kitty Wu, and they seem to fall in love with each other immediately.
In August 1969, all of Marco's money is exhausted and he has to leave his flat. He takes a small knapsack and Uncle Victor's clarinet, walks out of the building and is down and out in New York.

> "I turned south, paused for a moment, and then took a step. Then I took another step, and in that way I began to move down the street. I did not look back once." (p. 54)

These words clearly echo the famous first words of the first man on the moon, an event which coincides with Marco's personal disaster. "As chance would have it" (p. 38), Marco sells his last books on the day Neil Armstrong steps out onto the moon ("a small step for a man but a giant leap for mankind," Neil Armstrong, July 20, 1969). Marco can watch this scene in a small bar and joins in the guests' laugh at President Nixon's euphoric exaggeration that the moon landing is the greatest event since the creation of man. In an ironic reversal, the narrator expresses his critical view saying that "since the day he was expelled from Paradise, Adam had never been this far from home." (p. 39) In spite of the fact that Marco is an expert on literature about journeys to the moon, he keeps distance from the New York festivities in August 1969. Similarly, the social and political upheavals of the late sixties are of no real concern to Marco, who is only a very distant observer of the dramatic events: the student revolt, the assassinations of Martin Luther King (April 4, 1968) and Robert Kennedy (June 5, 1968), the division of the nation over the Vietnam War, President Johnson's announcement that he would not run for a second term (March 31, 1968), the conflicts in Prague and Berlin. These events are only marginal to Marco, as he is preoccupied with his personal crisis. Nevertheless, he sees a parallel between both spheres: "My own story stands in the rubble of those days, and unless this fact is understood, none of it will make sense." (pp. 25–26)
His personal disorder seems to be a reflection of the chaos of the world at large. If Marco is "out of step with the rest of the world" (p. 22), he is especially out of touch with the lifestyle and the general mood of his own generation. On the day he has to leave his flat, he happens to cast a glance at a large

photo in a newspaper, and with utter disbelief and great bewilderment he sees a picture of the immense mass of young people at Woodstock (August 15th–17th, 1969).

Chapter II

Marco in Central Park

At the beginning of this chapter the narrator again assumes a more general point of view moving freely back and forth in the chronological order of the story and giving direct comments on the events. Foreshadowing his rescue from his almost deadly crisis, he praises the power of love and shows his great gratitude to Zimmer and Kitty. Auster's use of metaphorical language with which Marco describes his precarious situation ("I had jumped off the edge of a cliff," p. 57) clearly alludes to Holden Caulfield (J. D. Salinger, *The Catcher in the Rye*) who sees his ideal personal task in preventing children from falling over cliffs.

Looking back, Marco describes how Zimmer and Kitty Wu fail to contact him despite repeated attempts.

It is August 1969 when Marco leaves his apartment at 112th Street. He walks south to avoid chance meetings with Columbia students and professors. Marco has no survival plan. He walks down to Columbus Circle finding a ten-dollar note there on the pavement. He is much assured by this, seeing it as a sign of a well-meaning fate. He walks on to 42nd Street near Times Square and around mid-afternoon goes into a cinema to escape from the hot and stifling weather. To him, it is again a clear sign of fate that the movie they show happens to be *Around the World in 80 Days*. It reminds him of the times with Uncle Victor, who had taken him to this movie eleven years before (at the age of eleven). On the one hand, he feels protected by the spirits of fate, on the other hand, however, he also feels great shame in his belief that he has disappointed Uncle Victor by turning himself "into a nothing" (p. 60).

He leaves the cinema in the early evening and wanders aimlessly around to finally seek shelter in Central Park at eleven o'clock at night. He lies down under a bush behind the 'Home' plate of a softball field, and to his surprise he soundly sleeps through the night. Central Park becomes his refuge and his new 'home'. He feels at ease here as he does not feel forced to adapt to the codes of behavior, dress and looks of the New York streets. He enjoys the solitude and the great freedom of the park: There is much greater tolerance towards all kinds of looks and behavior. Here he can concentrate on his thoughts and on himself without being disturbed by others or by activities which go along with normal everyday life. He lives from the food and drinks left behind by the many park visitors; sometimes he is invited to take part in picnics or is given leftovers from parties. Nevertheless, he feels humiliated when he is compelled to search the garbage cans to find something to eat. To keep his self-respect he attempts to see his lifestyle as a "challenge to the American way. [...] I was living proof that the system had failed, that the smug, overfed land of plenty was finally cracking apart." (p. 68) Life in Central Park is not without dangers for Marco, but they turn out to be harmless. Once he stumbles over three people having sex under the bushes and is attacked by them, but he escapes. In another incident a mentally deranged man takes Uncle Victor's clarinet and tries to run away with it; Marco manages to get hold of him and reclaim his only possession. In spite of all the difficulties of life in the park, Marco seems to recover a bit from his tormenting self-absorption. He stays in contact with what is going on in the world by reading the newspapers left behind in the park. He learns about Senator Edward Kennedy's mysterious accident at Chappaquidick, the second moon landing of Apollo 12 and the sensational victory of the New York Mets over the Chicago Cubs. He compares the spectacular fall of the Chicago Cubs at the end of the season to his own situation. He becomes convinced that constant change is the main force of life.

For the first few weeks Marco could enjoy the dry and pleasant weather of late summer, also known as "Indian Summer". Then the weather changes and one day he gets thoroughly drenched by a heavy and lasting rain and visits a café and a public library to warm up and dry his clothes. In the café, Marco dries his hair under an electric sani-blower which results in a ridiculous, tower-like hairstyle. He takes his razor out of his knapsack and shaves off his hair, thereby changing his appearance so radically that he hardly recognizes himself in the mirror. On his way back to the park, he feels the fever rising; he has to vomit and with his last strength he manages to find refuge in a cave in Central Park. Before he loses consciousness, he is plagued by wild dreams and visions. He imagines he sees the MOON PALACE sign which is suddenly reduced to two O's only. They turn into two gigantic human eyes "that were looking down at me with scorn and impatience. They kept on staring at me, and after a while I became convinced that they were the eyes of God." (pp. 76–77) After two or three days, Marco crawls out of the cave into the warm sun, endlessly uttering the words "Indian Summer". Lying there, he starts dreaming of Indians, the native Americans. In his fantasy, he follows a group of Indians through the forest of Manhattan some 350 years ago. He becomes aware of the image of a girl with a Navaho headband. She is bending over him and Marco seems to recognize her and calls out her name: POCAHONTAS. In reality the girl with the Indian headband is Kitty Wu, who together with Zimmer has finally succeeded in tracking down Marco and saves his life, just as Pocahontas saved the life of Captain John Smith some 350 years ago.

Chapter III

Marco's recovery – the physical – in love with Kitty Wu

David Zimmer gives Marco a temporary home in his small flat to help his friend recover from his physical and psychic exhaustion. Zimmer provides food, leaves his bed to Marco and does all he can to make Marco find his balance again. Nevertheless, Zimmer vehemently reproaches Marco for not having asked for help when he was in need of it. Marco realizes that it was not courage but cowardice and selfishness which made him avoid help and instead begin this course of self-destruction. In his great remorse for having offended his friends and the people around him, Marco decides to make a new start. He plans to reverse his attitude totally, to leave behind his self-absorption and to achieve instead "a state of total selflessness" (p. 80) towards his friends and surroundings.

When Marco has partially recovered, he takes a look at his possessions, and comes across the letter from the draft board which summons him to a physical examination on the 16th September. As Marco has completely lost track of date and time and assumes that it must be later than September, he is greatly surprised and relieved that it is exactly the day before this ominous date. In spite of his physical weakness and mental instability, Marco insists on keeping this appointment for fear of being taken to prison as a draft dodger.

Unlike many of the young men of his generation, he has not prepared any strategy to be found unfit for military service. In Zimmer's clothes and still exhausted from illness and malnutrition he undergoes the various procedures of the physical. With a hundred young men he first fills in some forms. Here, he naïvely states that he once belonged to some left-wing organizations during his high school and college years. He has become so thin that the doctors can hardly take blood from his shrunken veins; he is measured and weighed ("112 pounds, I think it was, or perhaps 115" – about 50 respectively

53 kilograms, p. 84) He is separated from the group of young men and sent to a psychiatrist. He openly answers a row of intimate questions, surprising the psychiatrist when he can convince him that he does not take drugs. After this formal examination the psychiatrist conducts a more personal conversation. Marco freely presents his whole story trying to make the army doctor understand his motives for dropping out. He tries to explain to this somewhat sober doctor that "because I thought that by abandoning myself to the chaos of the world, the world might ultimately reveal some secret harmony to me, some form or pattern that would help me to penetrate myself." (p. 86) With a mixture of pity and incomprehension the doctor interrupts Marco's long monologue, and fills in a form declaring him unfit for military service. The commanding officer is much relieved by this because otherwise he would have been forced to go through a lengthy investigation into Marco's left-wing activities. Before he receives his final papers, Marco has to wait in a room where all the 'rejects' have come together. He finds himself grouped together with "the simpletons, the grotesques, the young men who did not belong anywhere." (p. 87)

In the second half of September, Marco recovers rapidly and begins to regain his weight. In the evenings, Zimmer and Marco often go to a small bar, where they can have light meals, watch TV and talk to each other. Zimmer praises Kitty Wu's qualities and tells a disbelieving Marco that she is in love with Marco; he maintains that, because of her great reserve, it is Marco who must make the first move. During one of these long conversations Zimmer tells Marco all he needs to know about Kitty's family and her emigration to the USA. Kitty's father was a Kuomintang general in the revolutionary wars. He followed Chiang Kaishek to Taiwan, where Kitty was born in 1950 – not to General Wu's wife, but to his second concubine. General Wu was appointed ambassador to Japan, and the whole family, including Kitty, moved there. Kitty spent her childhood in Tokyo enjoying privileges like American schools, ballet lessons and chauffeur-driven cars. When Kitty was 14 years old, her mother died and Kitty was sent to the USA to a boarding school in Massachusetts. She attended Fielding Academy (a dance and ballet school) for four years and then enrolled in the famous ballet school Juilliard in New York. When she meets Marco, she is due to start her second year there.

Marco has recovered and therefore insists on Zimmer taking his own room and bed again while he sleeps on the floor. In return for Zimmer's kindness, Marco takes over one of his jobs: the translation from French into English of a 100-page document concerning the restructuring of the French embassy. He sees this tedious work as a kind of penance for all his past mistakes, and works dutifully on it for almost a month. One afternoon in mid-October, he quite by chance meets Kitty Wu again in a small park. At once there is harmony and understanding in their conversation. Marco invites her to Zimmer's room. They confess their love to each other and make love. In retrospect Marco describes this experience as "an earthquake in the heart of my solitude." (p. 99) Marco and Kitty enjoy their relationship even if they have difficulty in finding suitable places for their love-making. Marco finishes the translation by the end of October and with his pay Marco, Zimmer and Kitty meet to celebrate and have dinner in the MOON PALACE.

> "It was a superb moment for me, a moment of astonishing joy and equilibrium, as though my friends had gathered there to celebrate my return to the land of the living." (p. 101)

Marco's fortune cookie contains a message saying "The sun is the past, the earth is the present, the moon is the future." (pp. 101–102) Marco starts looking for a job and is soon successful. An elderly man in a wheelchair takes him as a live-in companion to help him along with his daily walks and his secretarial work. So Marco leaves Zimmer and moves to Thomas Effing's house at the corner of West End Avenue and Eighty-fourth Street.

Chapter IV

Marco becomes Effing's companion – Effing's life story (part 1)

On November 1st, the "Day of the Dead" and all "unknown saints" (p. 103), Marco Fogg goes to Thomas Effing's West Side apartment, which overlooks the Hudson, to be interviewed for the job. He is welcomed by Mr. Effing's nurse and housekeeper, Mrs. Rita Hume. She leads him to the eighty-six-year-old man. Effing appears to be blind as he is wearing black patches over his eyes. Effing starts the interview asking pointed and surprising questions, e.g. "Are you a man of vision?", "When you see a thing before your eyes, are you able to identify it?" (p. 105)
Marco's open but cautious answers seem to find Effing's approval. He feels Marco's muscles to see if he is strong enough to wheel him along the streets. Effing is satisfied and employs Marco, but warns him that he will have a difficult time with him and that he might even hate him.
The next morning, Marco takes the few things he has from Zimmer's room to Effing's apartment. He says good-bye to Zimmer. He will not see his best

friend again except in a chance meeting in 1982 in lower Manhattan. The narrator, Marco Fogg, goes on to relate the details of that meeting at this point of the novel. There is no reason given why Marco has not stayed in contact with his closest friend: "Circumstances pulled us apart." (p. 109) Nevertheless, this chance meeting is given as the reason why he came to write down the story of his youth. "I suspect that the idea to write this book first came to me after that meeting" (ibid.).

In Effing's apartment, Marco has his own sparsely furnished room, which he compares to a monk's cell. He develops ambivalent feelings of hate and respect towards this strange old man:

> "He was a monster, but at the same time he had it in him to be a good man, a man I could even bring myself to admire." (p. 120)

On some days, Effing is full of nastiness, bitterness and sarcasm, making life difficult for the unshakable Mrs. Hume and a confused Marco Fogg. Effing also displays disgusting habits, probably to derive some perverse pleasure from shocking his companions. He likes "letting the food dribble out of his mouth and down the chin, burping, feigning nausea and heart attacks, removing his false teeth and putting them on the table" (pp. 113), slurping the soup with an awful noise. On the other hand, Marco Fogg is fascinated by Effing's strong will and his keen intellectual interest in manifold subjects. During the first two days in Effing's service, Marco has to read aloud several books dealing with travel into the unknown and the discovery of new worlds. Sometimes Marco gets the feeling that Effing has a strategy in mind to pass on some special knowledge to him, to initiate him into the secrets of the world. He plays the role of a secret mentor and master. Effing loves to surprise Marco. So sometimes he does not wear his black patches over his eyes, but dark sunglasses, or a black headband, or spectacles or nothing at all. In this way he confuses Marco, who in spite of the long time he stays with Effing is not sure whether the man is blind or not.

When the sun comes out on his third day in Effing's service, Effing is carefully fitted out for an outing into the streets of Manhattan. In his right hand he has a stick enabling him to give his orders to Marco. On this and further excursions, Effing asks Marco to describe the objects he points at. Accompanied by Effing's curses, Marco is forced to develop a method of precisely describing everyday objects like garbage cans, doorways, the clouds in the western sky so that Effing has a clear and concrete image of reality. Marco considers this task as a possibility to learn "humility, patience, rigor" (pp. 121–122) and as a spiritual exercise to put reality and the world in words. He learns to restrict the description of objects to significant details only, to avoid piling too many words on top of each other, and to simplify his sentences. Effing in his wheelchair is a well-known figure in his neighborhood because for more than thirty years he was wheeled around there by Marco's predecessor, Pavel Shum. Effing's favorite place is Riverside Park where he can enjoy nature. He asks Marco to identify and describe the plants he sees.

Effing carefully prepares Marco for his major project, namely to write down his own obituary. Effing thinks it is about time to do this as he senses that he will die soon. He thinks it necessary to prepare his own obituary because some 40 years ago when, after his disappearance, people thought he had died, the obituary that appeared in the newspaper did not, in his opinion, do him justice as a man and a painter. He tells Marco that he was a "great American painter" in his youth.

In spite of Effing's announcement, he does not start with his dictation and report the following day. Instead, Effing quizzically presents details about the life of the well-known American painter, Ralph Albert Blakelock. Effing tells Marco that he knew Blakelock personally quite well and that Blakelock had had a great influence on his life. Blakelock once traveled out West completely on his own and stayed in Indian territory for three years, creating a series of paintings depicting the vanishing Wild West. After returning home, Blakelock became mentally ill and was shut up in an asylum, while his pictures sold at unheard-of sums. One painting called *Moonlight* (1885) was bought for 14,000 dollars by a senator, "the highest price ever paid for the work of a living American artist." (p. 134) As Marco Fogg – to Effing's deep contempt – has never heard of Blakelock, Effing sends him to the Brooklyn Museum to intensively study the Blakelock painting Moonlight and memorize it. "Imagine that you are Blakelock, painting the picture yourself." (p. 137) When he finally sees the small dark painting in the Brooklyn Museum he cannot help feeling disappointed. The painting is only 27 by 32 inches (68.58 by 81.28 cm) large, it has little color – it is dark and brown – and does not present anything dramatic at all.

It is a calm landscape picture with a perfectly round full moon in the middle of it, illuminating the objects around: the sky, a lake, a large tree in the foreground, the low mountains on the horizon and on the left the Indian teepee, a campfire and a few Indians. The longer he studies the picture, however, the better he can appreciate it, and understand its meaning. In a time when the last patches of primeval America were disappearing, when the massacre at Wounded Knee signaled the end of Indian freedom, Blakelock tried to portray "[…] an American idyll, the world the Indians had inhabited before the white men came to destroy it. [...] this picture was meant to stand for everything we had lost. It was not a landscape, it was a memorial, a death song for a vanished world." (p. 140)

Marco returns home from the museum, but Effing does not show up. So Marco goes to the Columbia art library to verify the details Effing presented about Blakelock's life and his paintings. He sees that most things Effing has told him are correct.

Without referring to Blakelock again, the following morning Effing starts relating his life story. He does not begin with his birth and family, but jumps right to the middle, telling Marco that at the age of 26/27 he spent most of his time painting in Shoreham on Long Island. Here, he was in close contact with Thomas Moran, another well-known American landscape painter. Moran, who himself had been to the West several times to depict it for the people in the East, motivated Effing to follow his footsteps and go West. Effing goes back a step in his life story and turns to Tesla, the rival of Edison. Some chance meetings with Tesla had left a deep impression on him and he even claims that a look in Tesla's eyes made him understand what mortality was. He claims that it was Tesla's eyes which persuaded him to become a painter. He then presents his personal story of the rivalry of Tesla and Edison to reveal his critical attitude towards technological progress. He is full of sarcasm about man's belief in being master of nature. To him, progress was a destructive and futile power. One day it would blow up the whole world and lead to technological nonsense: "A bigger and better mousetrap every month. Pretty soon, we'll be able to kill all the mice at the same time." (p. 148) In spite of his father's resistance Effing stuck to his sudden decision and became a painter. When his very wealthy father died – he had earned his money on Wall Street – he was very rich. To end his personal story of Tesla, Effing relates a much later incident when he saw a mentally confused Tesla feeding the pigeons in a park. The one time genius and 'prophet of the future' had become a broken-down old man and a bum.

After this, Effing is set to present the story of his second life in great detail. Although Effing did not regard himself as a traditional and romantic landscape painter, he followed Moran's example to experience the vast wide spaces and open skies of the West. In 1912, Effing married, but his marriage was a failure. He suffered from the frigidity of his wife, and so he saw in this another reason to go West. He found a young and spirited companion, Edward Byrne, who wanted to become a topographer and surveyor. Both fully equipped, they started on their expedition in 1916. They went to Salt Lake City by train, hired a scout, Scoresby, and set out for the wilderness. They entered the Great Salt Desert and were overwhelmed by the empty and dead world. Effing felt strongly motivated and drew a great number of pictures. They moved on to Nevada, traveled along the Confusion Range of the Rocky Mountains and experienced the extreme whiteness of snow and clouds and the unearthly silence in the mountains. Effing felt oppressed by the enormous space and the emptiness of the country. "It was like being locked in a prison [...]. The land is too big out there, and after a while it starts to swallow you up." (p. 157) They finally reached the fantastic area of the Four Corners where Utah, Arizona, Colorado and New Mexico meet. They walked around the canyons and visited the cliff dwellings of the pre-Columbian Anasazi. During the journey Mr. Scoresby, the guide, grew more and more hostile, the mood in the group deteriorated as a donkey had to be shot and the water supply got scarce. On the way to the town Bluff, Scoresby suggested a short cut, but the terrain soon became very difficult, causing Byrne's horse to slip, and together they fell over a cliff three hundred feet down into a valley. Scoresby killed the injured horse and departed, leaving Effing alone with his dying companion. After Byrne's death, Effing buried him and put a stick with a piece of paper on top of the grave which read: "Edward Byrne,1898–1916. Buried by his friend, Julian Barber" (p. 162).

Chapter V

Effing's life story (part 2) – Effing's final days and death

Whereas in Chapter IV Effing tells his story directly in the form of a monologue, in Chapter V the continuation of Effing's story is narrated by Marco. This form gives the narrator Marco the freedom to comment on Effing's behavior and actions.

After Byrne's death, Effing wandered around in the canyon, crying about the loss of his young companion and his own failure not to prevent Byrne's death. His horse collapsed on the second day and his food and water supplies ran out. To add to the desperate situation, Effing soon realized that his shame about the course of events and his loss of face had made it impossible for him to return home again. Here, it became clear to him that he would have to give up his identity as Julian Barber. Effing found a cave near the top of a cliff which gave him shelter and thus saved his life. Marco is surprised about the parallels with his life story and his time in the cave of Central Park. As a consequence, he develops sympathy for Effing and his fate. Marco cannot "help thinking of him as a kindred spirit." (p. 181) In contrast to the cave in Central Park, Effing's cave was large and furnished with a table, a couple of chairs, a cupboard, a bed and a stove and contained a large store of food. When Effing had a closer look at the bed he found a man in it, who had been shot in the right eye. He buried the man some forty feet down from the cave beside a brook where the ground was soft. Effing decided to take on the identity of this solitary cave dweller. He wanted to stay there as long as possible to make his family and friends think that he had died on his expedition to the West.

After two weeks of extreme changes of mood he became increasingly balanced. To make the food provisions last as long as possible, he worked out a detailed plan and from then on he stuck to it. When one night he was writing his daily entry in his diary, he spontaneously started drawing. This was the beginning of a new daily routine. He went out every day, painting pictures all day long in the open air. He did so for two and a half months till all his colors had been used up. Working hard to represent the landscape around him on canvas helped him to cope with the enormous emptiness and the vast spaces around him. He was no longer afraid of these gigantic surroundings, on the contrary, he felt at ease in this life of isolation and solitude. He felt sure that this was the happiest period of his life.

One day, seven months after he had taken possession of the cave, an Indian appeared and greeted him as his "old friend Tom." Effing soon realized that the Indian mistook him for the killed man and therefore cleverly slipped into this role. The Indian named Ugly Mouth George was a bit simple and so it was easy for Effing to learn the most important details about Tom and not betray himself. He found out that a quarrel had been going on between Tom, the cave dweller, and the Gresham brothers, a dangerous band of Western outlaws. Effing realized that the lonely hermit Tom had been killed by these gunmen. The Indian's visit destroyed Effing's illusion of being able to live in perfect peace and solitude. It was clear now that people could find him, and he had to be on his guard because he was sure that the Gresham brothers would return to the cave. His peace of mind vanished as "the harmony of his world was destroyed." (p. 175) He carefully prepared himself for the visit of the Gresham brothers. He left the cave, slept in the open and removed as far as possible all personal traces from the cave. After two months, in the middle of May (one year after he had left New York), the Greshams came riding up to the cave. The three men went into the cave, preparing things to stay there for the night. In the middle of the night when everything was quiet, Effing cautiously entered the cave and in great cold-bloodedness managed to kill all three. The following morning he buried them beside the hermit Tom. He searched their saddle bags and found more than 20,000 dollars, several watches, bracelets, necklaces and three packets of bonds worth about another 10,000 dollars. Effing did not spare a single thought about returning the money; he would take it to start a new life. Moreover, he did not feel a sting of conscience about having committed murder. He left his paintings and his notebooks behind in the cave, took enough food and water and rode away with the three horses of the Gresham brothers.

Effing made his way to San Francisco where he adopted the name of Thomas Effing: Thomas – after the painter Thomas Moran and the hermit Tom, and Effing going back to the associations of *doubting Thomas* (Bible) and *fucking Thomas* which is finally reduced to the more acceptable *f-ing = Effing*. This then was to become his new surname. "Thus, he was Thomas Effing, the man who had fucked his life." (pp. 182–183)

In San Francisco, Effing became very wealthy within nine months by investing the robbers' money on the stock market. He bought a large house, had servants and was accepted in the best circles of society. At a dinner party one night however, he was confronted with a former colleague of his father's who recognized him but was persuaded by Effing that this other man must have been his perfect double. Nevertheless, this party guest told everybody at the party the strange story of the disappearance of a man called Julian Barber. This was a strong warning for Effing and from that day on he withdrew from public life and avoided contact with the social circles of San Francisco. For several months he shut himself away in his house, only leaving it at night to seek all kinds of doubtful pleasures in Chinatown (prostitutes, gambling, opium). Effing developed a deep contempt at what he had made of his life and he thought it was best to lead an immoral life as he was a sinner anyway. He spent almost a third of his wealth on the excesses of these few months. One night, on his way back home from Chinatown, he was attacked by a stranger for no apparent reason. He was given a tremendous blow on his head, collapsed and was sliding down a steep slippery street until he crashed into a lamp-post, which broke his spine and left his legs unmovable. He understood this accident as a just punishment for his crimes given by heaven, the more so as this blow had been dealt to him out of the blue. He had not seen the attacker and he did not know why he had been attacked. After his recovery, which took nine months, Effing sold his house, transferred his money to a Swiss bank, bought a false passport under the name of Thomas Effing and went to Paris in 1920. As a young man he had spent a year in Paris and could speak French well. From an earlier passage of the novel the reader knows that in Paris Effing was cared for by Pavel Shum. They left France in 1939 and went back to the USA to live in New York. With this, Thomas Effing ends his autobiography.

Effing tells Marco to work out three different "obituaries" from these accounts: a short version of 500 words for the newspapers, a more sensational version of 3000 words for an art magazine and then an edited version of the complete transcript.

By the beginning of March 1970, Marco has finished his job of editing and typing these three reports. With this job done, he one morning finds three history books on his bed – books written by the historian Solomon Barber. Marco rightly assumes that Solomon Barber is Julian Barber's (i.e. Thomas Effing's) son. Some time after his return to New York, Thomas Effing discovered he had a son and with the help of Pavel Shum he found out about his son's life. Solomon Barber was born in 1917, nine months after Effing had left for the West. Effing's wife and Solomon's mother died in 1939, the year Effing came back to New York. Solomon Barber became a historian and a professor at small colleges. To make up to his son Solomon Barber and to recognize him as such, Effing makes a will leaving him his money after his death. He might have had a bad conscience for never having wanted to meet him when he was back in New York.

> "I'm going to leave him my money. [...] The poor sap's made such a hash of his life, maybe it will do him some good. He's a fat, childless, unmarried, broken-down wreck, a walking dirigible disaster." (p. 194)

Effing instructs Marco to give Solomon Barber the long version of his life story after his death and to make sure that Solomon Barber receives his money. When Marco shows his surprise at Effing mentioning his death, Effing even predicts the date of his death: he will die in two month's time, on May 12th. With his obituaries written, Effing loses his vitality and interest in his surroundings. One morning after three weeks of brooding – it happens to be April 1st – he comes up with an eccentric plan. In spite of Mrs. Hume's protests, Effing is going to distribute 20,000 dollars in fifty-dollar bills at random to passers-by in the streets of New York. The Gresham brothers stole 20,000 dollars from anonymous strangers, and having made a lot of money out of this sum during his life, he is going to give it back to anonymous people. Before his death, he wants to do a final deed of penance. For several days, Marco wheels Effing through the streets of New York giving money to those who look as if they could need it. On the last day of this spectacular project, it is extremely rainy and windy. Effing insists on going out to finish the job. He makes a great show of this last outing in the rain and wind: he holds up an umbrella, but it does not have any cloth to protect him from the downpour of rain.

> "This was to be his last night, and he wanted to go out in a frenzy, to bring his own death down on himself as his final, glorious act." (p. 209)

Completely drenched from the rain, they go into a dirty café and throw the last five or six fifty-dollar bills at the customers. During this bizarre outing, Marco Fogg's and Effing's relationship changes fundamentally. Marco sees that Effing wants to die and, with great empathy, he does not stand in the way of his final wish. Effing catches a severe cold and fatal pneumonia. He has to stay in bed, cared for by a doctor and a nurse. Marco spends every day with him in his room while Effing holds his hand.

> "Since the rainstorm, our relationship had changed to such an extent that he now doted on me as if I were his own flesh and blood." (p. 213)

On the evening of May 11th, Marco goes out to dinner with Kitty at the Moon Palace and afterwards to the movies. Marco worries about Effing and therefore goes home only to find out that Effing has just died: on May 12th, 2 minutes after midnight.
According to Effing's instructions, his body is to be cremated and his ashes are to be scattered in the waters of New York harbor. Marco Fogg cannot inform Solomon Barber about his father's death before the funeral because the professor has gone on a research trip to England. So Marco writes a letter to inform Solomon Barber about Julian Barber's second identity. He encloses Effing's long autobiography and sends it to the history department of his college. Two days after Effing's death, Marco and Mrs. Hume fetch Effing's urn from the mortuary and together with Kitty and Mrs. Hume's brother they go onboard the Staten Island Ferry. As soon as they approach the Statue of Liberty, Marco opens the urn and scatters the ashes. Back at Effing's house, Marco says good-bye to Mrs. Hume. At the last moment, she remembers to hand him a brown grocery bag in Mr. Effing's name. Kitty peers in, begins to smile and turns it upside-down. "An endless shower of old rumpled bills" (p. 223) pours out, leaving Marco the fortune of more than seven thousand dollars.

Chapter VI

Solomon Barber's life story – Marco leaves Kitty

For the following months Marco leads a life of great happiness. Together with Kitty, he rents a dusty loft in an old warehouse on East Broadway right in the middle of Chinatown. With Effing's money, the young couple buy a stove and a refrigerator, they collect discarded furniture from the streets, install the barest necessities in the bathroom and settle down.

Kitty can use the huge space (2,000 square feet) to practice her dancing. Kitty does not want to be financially dependent on Marco, so she takes up a job with a publishing company during her long summer vacations. As she works there from nine to five, Marco, who has not taken up another job, takes care of the housework, cooking and shopping. "[...] perhaps two or three months after we started living together, I think we both began to suspect that we were heading toward marriage." (pp. 226–227) In mid-September – four months after Effing's death – Solomon Barber contacts Marco by mail and suggests a meeting in New York in early October. Marco meets him in a hotel lobby and is confronted with a monstrously fat man. Even in the opening conversation between the two men, the reader learns that Solomon Barber once had a brilliant young student called Emily Fogg at Oldburn College, Ohio.

At this point, the reader correctly suspects that Solomon Barber is Marco's father (and that Thomas Effing, alias Julian Barber, is Marco's grandfather). Marco, however, does not see the family connection. As the retrospective narrator, on the other hand, he is able to tell us about Solomon Barber's affair with his mother, details that Marco really finds out about at a later stage in the novel. In his first college post at Oldburn College, Ohio, Solomon Barber falls in love with the best student of his freshman class. It is Emily Fogg. They are found out the first time they sleep together, and because of the scandal both have to leave college. He proposes to Emily to marry her, but she rejects him, and flees home to Chicago. Emily never tells anyone about this affair and after her son Marco is born never reveals the identity of her lover and son's father to anybody. Solomon Barber has no knowledge of his fatherhood and does not know where Emily Fogg lives.

The reader is now told the story of Solomon Barber's childhood and youth, in which the narrator jumps back and forth in time. Solomon Barber is born nine months after his father's disappearance in the West (1917) and lives together with his mother and various maids in the large house in Shoreham, Long Island. He grows up fast to his full adult size; at the age of 15 he is six foot three inches tall (about 1.90 m). From that time on, he puts on weight and soon weighs more than 250 pounds (about 113 kg). Suffering from this abnormality he seeks refuge in books. He is an outstanding high school student who graduates first in his class. He leaves for New York to spend four years at Columbia University to study history. Because of his enormous size – meanwhile he weighs about 290 pounds (about 132 kg) – he is rejected by the army. He finishes his studies successfully, and because of his prize-winning thesis ("Bishop Berkeley and the Indians") he is offered several positions at renowned universities. However, he accepts the post at the small college in Ohio, where, in his first year, he has his affair with Emily Fogg. From then on, Solomon Barber restlessly moves from college to college in the West and Midwest, never staying longer than two years at one place. He is a recognized historian and very popular with his students, but due to his still increasing weight – he is the "fattest professor" anyone has seen – and because of his appearance he is not accepted at elite colleges in the East. He cultivates his oddness, for instance by wearing a different hat each day. In 1959, Solomon Barber's academic journeys take him to Saint Paul, Minnesota, where, at that time, Uncle Victor and Marco are also living. Solomon Barber one day sees Victor Fogg's ad offering clarinet lessons and decides to contact him in the hope of finding information about Emily Fogg, the only woman he has loved in his life. Uncle Victor informs Solomon Barber about Emily's death. Uncle Victor, who senses that this man might be Marco's father, fears losing Marco. To avoid further contacts and chance meetings with Solomon Barber, he takes Marco and, without delay, leaves Saint Paul for Chicago – a missed chance for Marco to find out about his father:

> "[...] if Victor had answered Barber's second letter instead of running away, I might have discovered who my father was as far back as 1959." (p. 245)

At this point the narrator goes back again to Barber's childhood and adolescence. As a boy, Solomon learned various reasons for his father's disappearance but he knew that he had been a painter, which was quite evident for the boy as there were a great number of landscape paintings by his father in his home. Even as a young boy, Solomon Barber was very interested in his father's paintings and he was impressed by the two Blakelock pictures his family owned. In his third high school year he organized an exhibition about his father's paintings, distributing an essay he had written about his father's work.

Solomon Barber's mother had become mentally deranged soon after Solomon's birth. She never left her room and was cared for by a number of nurses and maids. As a young boy Solomon could only see his mother on special visits arranged by the nurses.

> "Miss Forrest set aside one hour for him every Thursday; Miss Caxton examined his fingernails before letting him in [...]. Once, Barber played dress-up with his mother for an entire afternoon, and on another occasion they sailed a toy boat in the pond until it got dark. Those [...] must have been the happiest hours he spent with her." (p. 247)

When Barber was seventeen, he wrote a novel called *Kepler's Blood,* in which he tried to cope with his father's disappearance and absence. In the following pages (pp. 249–262) Marco retells the story of Solomon Barber's novel. This 'book within a book' is a wild mixture of the most improbable events, but it contains the main elements of the novel proper: losing and finding one's father, guilt and penance, going West, primeval Indian cultures. These elements are to be seen as parallels reflecting and parodying the main events. The protagonist is John Kepler, a thirty-five-year-old artist who leaves his family in Long Island to go on a six-month trek through Utah and Arizona. John Kepler falls from a cliff, is severely injured, but saved by Indians who belong to a strange, primitive tribe. Kepler is greeted by them as their long lost savior and stays with them. When John Kepler's son is eighteen he decides to look for his father in the West and he manages to find him. Kepler senior rejects his son.

> "I am a spirit man who came here from the moon [...] and these people are the only family I have ever had." (p. 254)

Kepler junior is so disappointed about this that he kills his father the following night. He goes back to New York to become a successful business man. After some time, one of Kepler's Indian sons feels he has to avenge his father. Under the name of Jack Moon he travels to New York, but instead of killing Kepler Jr. he abducts Kepler Jr.'s son and takes him home to his tribe. John Kepler Jr., who is forty years old by now, again makes the long journey to Utah to find his son. Approaching the area,

> "[...] he [Kepler] suddenly sees a coyote standing with its silhouette against the moon. Fearful of everything in this remote and barren territory, Kepler impulsively points his rifle at the animal and pulls the trigger. The coyote is killed with one shot [...]. What he does not realize, of course, is that he has just killed his own son. Before he has time to stand up and walk over to the felled animal, three other coyotes leap out at him from the darkness. Unable to defend himself against their attack, he is chewed to pieces within a matter of minutes." (p. 257)

This is the fantastic story about a man who looks for his father, but kills him and finally even kills his own son. It is written by the young and immature Solomon Barber, who in this way tries to cope with the loss of his father.
The deranged Elizabeth Wheeler, Solomon Barber's mother and Effing's wife, dies in 1939. The only relative left to look after the house is Aunt Clara, a former vaudeville performer (and wife of Elizabeth Wheeler's brother) who is now addicted to sherry. Solomon Barber, who is not interested in his inheritance, leaves his family's house to Aunt Clara under the condition that after her death it will go to their black servant Hattie Newcombe. Before Solomon Barber leaves, he makes Aunt Clara tell him the details of his birth: When it was time for his mother to give birth to him, she became confused and refused to cooperate with the doctor and the midwife. She kept shouting that the baby was trying to kill her and that she would not let him out. After a long struggle, Solomon was delivered against his mother's will. He was the biggest, strongest baby anyone had ever seen. "More than eleven pounds [about 5 kg], the doctor said. A gigantus." (p. 265) From that day on, Mrs. Barber was mentally deranged. She thought she was a little girl and regarded her baby Solomon as her baby brother.
The narrator now resumes the basic time line of the novel again, going back to Solomon Barber's first stay in New York. Marco Fogg tells us how he says good-bye to Solomon Barber, at that time still not knowing that this eccentric man is his father. In spite of his colossal appearance, Marco is attracted to Solomon's personality, his humor and intellectual quality. Barber, however, is aware of their true relationship and when they say good-bye, his eyes fill with tears. "He was saying good-bye to his son, whereas I was merely seeing off a new friend [...]" (p. 266). When after some months they meet each other again, Barber tells Marco that he has inherited 46,000 dollars from Effing which will enable him to retire early. In their conversations it becomes clear that Barber has a plan for both of them. He wants to retrace the steps of his father he never knew. He plans to go on an expedition to Utah to see if the cave in which Effing spent a year and painted hundreds of pictures really exists. And he wants Marco and even Kitty to accompany him. Marco realizes the absurdity of the expedition suggested by Solomon, but it would provide him with an opportunity to get away from New York and his relationship with Kitty, which had taken a tragic turn.
Kitty has become pregnant, but to Marco's great disappointment and despair she does not want to have a baby yet. "[...] how could she go on dancing if she had a baby to take care of?" (p. 273) For Marco, the baby is a chance to overcome the loneliness of his childhood and to be finally part of a family.

He wants to become a father. But Kitty has her way. She finds a psychiatrist who is willing to state that she cannot give birth because she is in "mental endangerment" (p. 274), thus enabling her to have a legal abortion. Marco is shattered.

> "[...] I wound up spending several thousand dollars to destroy my own child. I was nearly broke again, and when I sat by Kitty's bed in the hospital and saw the drained and agonized look on her face, I could not help feeling that everything was gone, that my whole life had been taken away from me." (ibid.)

After the abortion, Marco wants Kitty to suffer for what she has done. At the same time he is upset about himself, how cruel he can be. Therefore he decides to leave her. He puts his last thousand dollars on the table, and in spite of Kitty imploring him not to leave her, he walks away.

Chapter VII

Marco finds and loses his father – the moon illuminates the darkness

Barber, who has rented an apartment in New York, puts up Marco. Marco finds a job with a small removal company and carries heavy furniture up and down flights of stairs everyday to get exhausted. In the evening he sits up late with Barber and drinks a bottle of wine to be able to get to sleep. Barber realizes that Marco is extremely unhappy about the breakdown of his relationship with Kitty and tries to reconcile them. Once he invites both to dinner in a restaurant without mentioning that the other would be there, too. When Kitty comes and sees Barber and Marco at a table, she turns around and goes home.
Although Marco is convinced that the project to go West with Barber to find Effing's cave is ridiculous, he keeps his promise to accompany Barber to Utah.

> "[...] the idea of a useless quest, of setting out on a journey that was doomed to failure, appealed to my sense of things at the moment. We would search, but we would not find. Only the going itself would matter, and in the end we would be left with nothing but the futility of our own ambitions. This was a metaphor I could live with, the leap into emptiness I had always dreamed of. I shook hands with Barber on it and told him to count me in." (p. 280)

They decide to go up to Chicago first to visit the grave of Marco's mother, Emily Fogg. Early in July 1971 Barber and Marco Fogg leave New York for the Midwest. Before they set out, Barber informs Kitty about this itinerary. Marco is in very low spirits and feels that his life come to a dead end. They drive up to Chicago in one day, so they are able to go to Emily Fogg's and Uncle Victor's graves the following day. Marco buys two bouquets, and after some difficulty they find the graves in Westlawn cemetery. At first, the two men cannot get near the graves as a team of four men are digging a grave for someone a few plots away from Emily's and Victor's graves. Then Marco can approach his mother's and his uncle's graves. He is overwhelmed by his feelings, and therefore does not notice what happens around him. In the Jewish fashion, he puts a stone on both his mother's and Uncle Victor's name plates. When after some time he turns around, he sees Barber weeping wildly and staring at the grave of Marco's mother. Barber expresses his deep love for Emily and his regret for all those wasted years. Marco begins to listen and suddenly all becomes clear: Solomon Barber is his father.

> "[…] the whole world began to rearrange itself before my eyes. He hadn't come out and said it, but all of sudden I knew. I knew who he was, all of a sudden I knew everything." (p. 284)

Marco's first reaction is fury; he swears and screams at Barber. Barber takes a few steps away from Emily's grave, loses balance and falls over backward into the freshly dug grave. As he is so enormous, he gets stuck in this grave. A crane is needed to lift him out of it. Barber is taken to hospital and operated on his back. He is confined to bed for two months. Marco visits him daily and spends eighteen or nineteen hours a day at his bed. Here, he has time to reconsider his identity and the way he sees himself. All his life he has seen his existence as a mystery. The unanswerable question of his origin has been a feature of his life. Now he knows who he is. However, he finds it difficult to accept his new identity. While lying in bed and suffering from his injuries, Barber's face undergoes a change. The cheeks become thinner, his face finer and a new look comes into his eyes. First Marco notices a resemblance to Effing's look and finally he realizes that he himself has the same eyes. "I was looking at myself." (p. 289) This helps him to accept that he is Barber's son. After two months, Barber dies and is buried next to Emily Fogg, in a plot which actually was destined for Marco. Marco persuades Mr. Green, the Rabbi who presided over his bar mitzvah, to conduct the funeral service for his father. No one except this rabbi and Marco himself is present at the funeral ceremony. Marco phones Kitty to be able to talk to someone and speak about this improbable story of finding and losing his father. Kitty is full of sympathy, but tells him that she is not willing to renew their relationship. After the funeral, Marco takes Barber's money and his car and heads out West. After a few days experiencing the vastness of the American continent, Marco arrives at the town of Bluff. His inquiries about Effing's cave, i.e. the cave of the Gresham Brothers, are successful and he is informed that the whole country has been flooded by Lake Powell, which was excavated two years before. Marco parks his car and hires a boat to cruise Lake Powell for a whole day. In the evening he returns, only to find out that his car with his inheritance of ten thousand dollars has been stolen. In an act of defiance he starts walking westward. Gradually his furious and desperate mood gives way to feelings of happiness and peace of mind. He keeps on walking for three months, heading towards the Pacific.

> "Once I reached the end of the continent, I felt that some important question would be resolved for me. […] I had only to keep walking to know that I had left myself behind, that I was no longer the person I had once been." (p. 297)

On January 6th 1972, Marco climbs over the hills into the town of Laguna Beach and walks down to the beach.

> "I had come to the end of the world, and beyond it there was nothing but air and waves, an emptiness that went clear to the shores of China. This is where I start, I said to myself, this is where my life begins." (p. 298)

On the beach he waits for the full moon to come up from behind the hills: "I kept my eyes on it as it rose into the night sky, not turning awy until it had found its place in the darkness." (ibid.)

Analysis and Interpretation

Setting

1. Place

The great mobility of all the major characters of the novel allows the writer to set his story in a range of places in New York, in the West, the Midwest and even in France. Everybody is constantly on the move. Solomon Barber tours the colleges of the Midwest, Uncle Victor goes on tour with his bands, Julian Barber alias Effing explores the West, ending up in California and finally in Paris, and Marco Stanley Fogg, the born traveller, follows Effing's footsteps to California after having gone through his spiritual odyssey in New York.
In *Moon Palace* Auster contrasts the urbanized East, where technological progress has its place, with the beauty and the wilderness of the West. The West once allowed the native Americans to live in harmony with nature. Even if at the time of the novel it has become a place of violence and crime, it still presents a challenge, and gives people the opportunity to start anew. The journey west to find one's identity follows the general course of American history in which the character of the USA was formed through the frontier experience.
In New York, Marco stays in a variety of places; they all have in common that they are only temporary and give him shelter for only a limited time. Marco stays in the college dormitory for just a term, he is evicted from his first student apartment, he stays in Central Park for a few weeks, he enjoys Zimmer's hospitality in his friend's small apartment from the end of September to the first of November, he lives in a small room at Effing's house from November to May, together with Kitty he lives in a loft for some months before he finally seeks refuge in Solomon Barber's hotel rooms for a few weeks. Most of these places are only small and narrow makeshift homes barely furnished. Marco often has just the basic necessities one needs in life. These places all seem to be part of experiments trying out the minimalist lifestyle. Whereas the rooms Marco stays at are characterized by a frustrating narrowness, Central Park offers openness and freedom from social control and psychological pressure.

> "It was live and let live, and as long as you did not actively interfere with what others were doing, you were free to do what you liked. There is no question that the park did me a world of good. It gave me privacy […]." (p. 64)

Marco is especially attracted by the ambivalent character of the park. A park belongs to the sphere of nature but at the same time it is man-made. Nevertheless, in his illness he needs a final retreat in a cave, which offers just the most basic necessity in life: shelter.
Central Park also represents a rehearsal or training for going west, a place to learn to understand people, to watch them as closely as possible. Later, Marco can use his experience when Effing talks to him about the West.
Cafés and restaurants are public places of sociability where one can meet friends and come into contact with people. Together with other people Marco watches the moon landing in a bar, his discussions and personal conversations with Zimmer take place in pleasant bar settings, the last of Effing's dollar bills are distributed in a coffee shop, which gives refuge from the rain which ultimately kills Effing, and the restaurant MOON PALACE makes the perfect setting for memorable events such as Marco's return to normal life.

> "I finished the translation at the end of October. Zimmer collected the money from his friend a few days later, and that night Kitty and I joined him for a meal at the Moon Palace. I was the one who chose the restaurant, more for its symbolic value than the quality of its food […]. It was a superb moment for me, a moment of astonishing joy and equilibrium, as though my friends had gathered there to celebrate my return to the land of the living." (p. 101)

2. Time

The period during which the novel mainly takes place (1965–1972) presents New York in the late sixties – a time of unrest and upheaval: the student revolts, the assassinations of Robert Kennedy and Martin Luther King, the national conflict about the escalating Vietnam War. There are also the first moon landing and the ups and downs of the Chicago Cubs and the New York Mets baseball teams. Marco sees this era as a time of disorder, which is reflected in his personal situation. For him, his personal crisis and the turmoil of his times are interrelated. By working Effing's story into the novel, Auster is able to cover almost a century of time. The vanishing peace and harmony of the American (i.e. Indian) West finds vivid expression in Blakelock's and Moran's landscape paintings, depicting America at the time of Custer's Last Stand and the massacre of Wounded Knee. Effing's contacts with Tesla and

Edison, for example at the Columbian Exposition in Chicago (1893), allow the narrator to illustrate the optimistic belief in technological progress of that time. When Effing returns to New York in 1940, he can comment on the World Fair, which has just started there, and give vent to his sarcasm on the state of the world.

> "Another hymn to progress, but it didn't do much for me this time, not after what I'd seen in Europe. It was all a sham. Progress was going to blow us up, any jackass could tell you that. You should meet Mrs. Hume's brother some time, Charlie Bacon. He was a pilot during the war. They had him out in Utah towards the end, training with that bunch that dropped the A-bomb on Japan. He lost his mind when he found out what was going on. The poor wretch, who can blame him?" (p. 148)

Later Marco learns from Charlie Bacon that his crew was expected to drop the bomb on Nagasaki.

> "There was no way they were going to get me to do that. Destruction on that scale is God's business. Men don't have the right to meddle in it. I fooled them by pretending to be crazy." (p. 220)

Charlie might be insane, but he plausibly maintains that in our time progress may lead to self- and mass-destruction.
There are many more hints at political and cultural events of American history; most of them are mentioned only in passing: e.g. the presidency of Theodore Roosevelt (p. 151), the First World War "the war to end all wars" (p. 131), the riots shortly after the First World War (the Palmer raids, the Sacco and Vanzetti case, p. 186), the Second World War and the German Occupation of Paris (p. 189), the destruction of Germany (p. 220), the McCarthy era (p. 239). All these references are presented from a rather critical perspective. Great events like D-Day, positive social developments under great presidents like F. D. Roosevelt, Kennedy and Johnson, e.g. the New Deal and the Civil Rights Movement have no place in Auster's novel.

Point of View

One of the most distinctive features of a fictional text is the writer's selection of the narrative perspective. The narrator and his point of view determine the presentation of the events and give literary form and meaning to the narration.

The first-person narrator of *Moon Palace* is Marco Fogg, the protagonist of the novel. He tells the story of the critical phase of his life; in addition to his personal crisis, he is also confronted with the life stories of two men who turn out to be his father and grandfather. The narrator tells his reader all the events he thinks to be relevant to understand his situation. He allows us to enter his mind as he presents his feelings, attitudes and thoughts. The fairly unlimited point of view in which he opens up his mind to us is contrasted with the limitations of an observer narrator whose perspective Marco adopts when he tells actions and describes the behavior of the other characters.

> "Effing was less combative than he had been during the interview, and for the most part he sat there in silence, listening to the books I read to him. It was difficult for me to judge the nature of the silence, whether he was using it to test me in a way I did not understand, or whether it was simply a reflection of his mood. As with so much of Effing's behavior during the time I stayed with him, I was torn between reading a dark purpose into his actions and dismissing them as the products of random impulse." (p. 111)

This passage clearly illustrates the double perspective of the first-person narrator: He allows the reader an unrestricted view of his mind whereas he is a limited narrator when he refers to the people and the world around. In some instances, Marco maintains that he has only a restricted capacity to present a complete picture of himself.

> "I can write down the things that happened to me, but no matter how precisely or fully I do that, those things will never amount to more than part of the story I am trying to tell." (p. 55)

The narrator is aware of his fundamental limitation restricting him to recognize only part of reality, even if it refers to himself.

> "There was a lot more, there must have been a lot more, but I can't pin down much of it. They gave us lunch somewhere (in the building? in a restaurant outside the building?), but the only thing I remember about the meal is that no one wanted to sit next to me." (p. 84)

Here it becomes clear that, on the whole, the limited point of view dominates. In this way Auster can express his general doubt about man to fully grasp reality and to reach truth.
The uncertainty and fundamental unreliability of the narrator to represent truth is reinforced by retrospective narration. Marco Fogg assumes a fairly late point of time (1986) from which he looks back, trying to remember his

troubles during adolescence and early adulthood. In some passages the narrator explicitly reminds the reader of the process of writing, which takes place much later than the action. Thus he can be vague about things, he can refer to his forgetfulness, and he can assume a critical distance towards his younger self ("Looking back on it now, I realize what a curious figure I must have cut", p. 22). Retrospection allows the narrator to select the details he thinks relevant. In addition, he can arrange events in the way which achieves the greatest effect. Thus, he freely makes use of foreshadowing (anticipation) to give the reader the final results of events in general terms before relating what happened chronologically and in details. This technique is impressively used at the beginning of the novel by anticipating the novel's essence and its outcome in a general and cryptic manner. In this way, the reader's interest is aroused and he/she feels appealed to by the narrator to read the whole story and find out what happens.

Although the narrator retells events chronologically from 1965 to 1972, in many passages he integrates extensive flashbacks from his childhood and, of course, the detailed reports about the lives of the men who turn out to be his father and grandfather. In spite of his restricted point of view, the narrator arranges the material in the order he thinks most appropriate for his story. He tells the reader that Solomon Barber is his father at a time when in reality Marco Fogg has not yet learned that this is so. And as the reader suspects this anyway due to various hints dropped by the narrator earlier on, he/she knows more than the acting narrator himself. This narrative technique allows the reader to fully comprehend the melodrama and the absurdity of the events at the grave of Emily Fogg.

Effing's life story is mainly presented by himself as a second narrator. In Chapter IV the story is related in monologue and direct speech. Marco, the narrator proper, becomes a listener and is in the same position as the reader. In this way, Effing is presented directly, as he wants to be seen, and not through Marco's eyes. In the following chapter, the narrator takes the initiative again and gives Effing's report in indirect speech. This allows him to give his personal comments and thoughts on Effing's Wild West experiences. The technique of just reporting on what someone else has said or written is employed again in the summary of Solomon Barber's juvenile novel *Kepler's Blood*. With this 'story within the story'/'book within the book' technique the reader cannot hold the narrator responsible for the implausible events. It is a feature of postmodern literature to unfold a text which itself opens up to further texts. This process of deconstructing a text has been compared to opening up a set of Russian Babushkas.

Mode of Presentation

Most of the novel is written in the mode of direct narration. Sometimes Auster employs a fairly scenic mode when the events are presented in great detail (e.g. the physical examination, Effing's accident in California, Marco's visit to Brooklyn Museum, Effing's life in the cave). In this way, great emphasis is placed on these events. A novel spanning almost over a century, however, can only be told if the action is condensed and presented in panoramic mode. So, for instance, Effing's life in France and in New York after his return are covered in only a few pages. Also Sol Barber's academic tour of colleges is dealt with only superficially. Even Marco's walk from Utah to California, which took three months and is crucial for his personal development, is told at great speed in only a few pages.

The narration is often characterized by a mood of reflection. This is due to the narrator's retrospective point of view. The events are often accompanied by the narrator's thoughts. He freely comments on what is going on, often from cultural or philosophical points of view. The novel displays Auster's great interest in various themes and makes Marco reflect on these: e.g. the workings of coincidence (p. 229), American continental expansion and its influence on the people and the character of the country (p. 140), and experimentation with minimalist lifestyles (pp. 36–37). The reflective mood can also be found in Effing's long monologue (Chapter IV, p. 141 ff), in which he freely conveys his personal thoughts on progress (p. 148) or on American landscape painting. As a counterbalance, Auster skillfully employs dialogue in various passages of the novel as a technique to make it livelier. In the short conversation between Marco and the caretaker Fernandez (pp. 52–53), Auster succeeds in bringing this simple but outspoken man to life. At the same time he depicts Marco as a young man who, in his defeat, shows considerable gallows humor and verbal skill. In his initial inability to understand how a well-educated young man like Marco can end up like a bum, Fernandez resorts to a somewhat naïve but deeply felt explanation:

> "Sometimes it's like everybody's gone crazy. If you wanna know what I think, it's those things they're shooting into space. All that weird shit, those satellites and rockets. You send people to the moon, something's gotta give. You know what I mean? It makes people do strange things. You can't fuck with the sky and expect nothing to happen." (p. 53)

Even the common man knows that man's hybris will be punished – a belief you can find throughout all ages. A humorous and sometimes biting tone is employed in the dialogues between Effing and Marco. In these passages the characters come more to life than in the long narrative parts. Whenever dialogue is used, the novel becomes lively, and the effect of the scenes is more direct. Here is an example in which Effing addresses Marco:

> "I don't suppose you've glanced at the books I left in your room on Tuesday," he said speaking as calmly as someone who had just requested another lump of sugar for his tea.
> "I've glanced at them," I said. "I've even gone so far as to read them."
> "You surprise me, boy. Considering your age, I'm beginning to think there might be some hope for you."
> "There's hope for everyone, sir. That's what makes the world go round."
> "Spare me the aphorisms, Fogg. What did you think of the books?" (p. 191)

Form and Structure

1. The main parts of the novel

The novel falls into three main parts. Each part focuses on the (also by way of flashbacks) life story of one of the main characters (see "Time Structure", pp. 48–49).

The first three chapters refer to Marco's life alone up to November 1st 1969. The narration covering his student days, his crisis, his life in Central Park, his rescue and recovery establishes a clear narrative line. The action is full of suspense and internal unity. This closely knit part helps the reader to identify with Marco and to feel pity for him.

Chapters four and five (second part) pursue Marco's steps from taking up service with Effing until Effing's death on May 12th 1970; in terms of structure, however, it is Julian Barber's or Thomas's life story which gives unity to this part.

Chapters six and seven (part three) again tell Marco's story, but the action is determined by the gradual revelation of details which first inform the reader and later reveal to Marco that Solomon Barber is Marco's father. The scene of father Solomon Barber's fatal fall clearly mark this passage as a culmination and turning point of the action. In a falling action, the last few pages show Marco cross the far West and reach the Pacific on January 6th 1972.

Time Structure

1965 – January 6th 1972 Marco Fogg's story (basic time of the action)	
1947	Marco Fogg is born
1958	his mother's death (Emily Fogg) Marco lives with Uncle Victor
1965	Marco starts to attend Columbia University
1966	Marco moves to his private apartment with Uncle Victor's books
1967	Uncle Victor's death
1969	August: Marco is evicted from his flat and stays in Central Park for 3 weeks (first moon landing: July 20, 1969) September: Kitty and Zimmer save Marco's life September 16th: Marco's army physical November 1st: Marco starts to work for Thomas Effing
1969–70	Marco stays in the service of Thomas Effing Effing tells him his life story
1970	May 12th: Effing dies June: Marco and Kitty take a flat together October: Marco becomes acquainted with Solomon Barber Barber tells him his life story
1971	March: Kitty becomes pregnant and has an abortion June: Marco separates from Kitty July: he sets out for the West with Solomon Barber September 4th: Barber dies October: Marco starts on his three-month walk to the Pacific
1972	January 6th: Marco watches the moon rise over the Pacific
1986	The narrator (Marco) tells the story

1883–1970 Julian Barber's / Thomas Effing's story	
1883	Julian Barber is born
1893	Columbian Exposition Chicago; meeting with Tesla
1905/06	Julian's father dies and he inherits millions, he becomes a painter influenced by Thomas Moran
1912	Julian marries Elizabeth Wheeler
1916	Julian leaves for his expedition to the West, sexual intercourse with his wife on the last night (Solomon Barber born in January 1917)
1916/17	Julian spends time alone in the cave
1917	May: Julian kills the Gresham brothers; June: Julian goes to California, takes up his new identity of "Thomas Effing"
1919	August: Effing's accident
1920	Effing goes to Paris
1939	Effing returns to New York, fleeing from the Nazis
1969	Effing hires Marco Fogg to write his obituary
1970	May 12th: Effing dies

1917–1971 Solomon Barber's story	
1934	Solomon Barber writes a novel to cope with his youth without a father
1939	His mother (Elizabeth Wheeler) dies, Barber attends Columbia University and becomes a historian
1946	Solomon Barber has an affair with his student Emily Fogg who becomes pregnant and gives birth to Marco Fogg in 1947
1950s–1960s	Barber teaches at various colleges in the Midwest
1970	October: Barber meets Marco Fogg and suspects that Marco is his and Emily's son
1971	September 4th: Solomon Barber dies

2. Parallelism – contrast – cycle

The structure of the novel is also determined by the principles parallelism, contrast and cycle. The life stories of the three main characters contain some striking parallels:

- Both Marco and Solomon grow up without a father although the fathers are still alive.
- All three men are restlessly on the move: Marco roams the small substitute world of Central Park and finally goes west after the unhappy end of his relationship to Kitty; Solomon Barber goes from college to college never staying longer than a few years at a place also because of an unhappy affair; Effing leaves his home and wife (after an unhappy marriage) for an expedition to the West, which eventually takes him to California, Paris and finally to New York, where he tours the streets in a wheelchair.
- Both Barber and Effing damage their backbones.
- Both Effing and Marco live in a cave for some time.
- Both Barber and Marco study at Columbia University.
- All three men have unhappy relationships with women and they are more or less to blame for the women's difficulties.
- All three men suffer from serious personal losses of some kind during their lives.

Within these parallels, the reader can easily detect obvious contrasts:

- Whereas Solomon Barber is an enormously fat man who suffers from obesity, Marco is at times extremely thin.
- All three men are very different in temperament: the ruthless and sarcastic Effing, the careful and thoughtful Barber, the sensitive and delicate Marco.
- Marco's retreat to Central Park and his three-day stay in a cave is only a superficial experience compared with Effing's escape to the West and his month-long existence in a cave.

Some of the similarities mentioned above are also reflected by other characters of the novel. Uncle Victor joins in the common restlessness. After an unhappy marriage he moves from town to town, he tours the West with his band and in the end he is a 'traveling' salesman selling encyclopaedias from door to door in Boise. In this way Auster reinforces the novel's parallelisms in the characters' movements.

Besides the parallels, the movements of the novel are to be seen as cyclical. Effing's life consists of various cycles, in each of which he vigorously overcomes disasters, finds success and ends up in a new disaster. He thinks that he has ruined his life. Likewise, Marco goes through cycles of crises and new beginnings. When one cycle ends, the next one begins. After his last crisis, he finds himself at the end of the world. As the moon rises and finds its position in the darkness of the sky, Marco sets his thoughts on a new beginning: "[...] this is where my life begins." (p. 298) The moon itself is a cyclical force which correspondingly influences human cycles. Many movements and cycles are determined by the time span of nine months (see "The magical figure 'nine'", p. 64), hinting at a natural origin and development of new life.

3. The picaresque character of the novel

> "The picaresque novel usually takes the form of a series of loosely connected episodes, frequently arranged as journeys and is often but not always autobiographical. It treats its subject realistically, with vivid details and plain if not earthy language. [...] Picaresque tales originated in sixteenth-century Spain. The best known Spanish tale is Miguel de Cervantes's *Don Quijote*. In England Daniel Defoe's *Moll Flanders* and Henry Fielding's *Tom Jones* represent the type. Mark Twain's *Huckleberry Finn* and Saul Bellow's *The Adventures of Augie March* are sometimes described as modern American picaresque novels."
> (*NTC Dictionary of Literary Terms*)

Moon Palace is certainly not a picaresque novel in the classical sense, but it shares various characteristics with this genre. Like so many of the picaresque heroes, Marco Fogg is an orphan: His mother dies young when he is eleven years old and his father is a complete mystery to him – there is not even a picture of him. He often sobbed himself to sleep "like some pathetic orphan hero in a nineteenth-century novel." (p. 10) The reader follows the hero in a series of episodic adventures. He is raised by an uncle, saved by friends from perishing in a cave, employed by a rich old man who turns out to be his grandfather, loved by a Chinese ballet student, supported by a colossal history professor who turns out be his father and who dies in a most improbable fashion. Marco crosses the continent and there, alone at the Pacific, the hero must feel orphaned many times over.

4. Journey of initiation

Closely linked with the picaresque form of the novel is Marco's journey to self-discovery, his quest for identity. The death of his uncle and the dwindling supply of money make Marco lapse into a deep personal crisis. He gradually loses contact with his surroundings. He is forced to recognize his total alienation from the world when he is completely at a loss to comprehend what is going on at Woodstock. Although the various elements of his name are used by him to establish his identity, the uprooted orphan does not know who he really is. He does not know his real origin and suffers from an identity crisis. This crisis makes him gradually retreat from the world and lead a life of contemplative introspection. He even progresses to self-abandonment. His situation becomes extremely desperate when starvation and illness lead to hallucinations and near madness.

> "Most of the time I was barely conscious and even when I seemed to be awake, I was so bound up in the tribulations of my body that I lost all sense of where I was. I remember long bouts of vomiting, frenzied moments when my body wouldn't stop shaking, periods when the only sound I heard was the chattering of my teeth." (p. 76)

All these elements – retreat to some backward area, starvation, hallucinations, vomiting, bodily pain – clearly hint at features commonly considered as parts of a painful initiation rite, the rites of passage. At the peak of his crisis Marco is metaphorically swallowed up by a cave and after three days belched or spat out again to be rescued.

> "I don't know how much time I spent in there. Two or three days, I would think, but it hardly matters now. When Zimmer and Kitty asked me about it, I told them three, but that was only because three is a literary number, the same number of days that Jonah spent in the belly of the whale." (ibid.)

The biblical and literary allusions encourage the reader to see Marco's crisis as an initiation process and the events in Central Park as symbolic of death and rebirth. Marco's crisis and rescue assume further religious overtones when, in his hallucination, he sees the neon sign of the MOON PALACE which is gradually reduced to MOON and finally to OO symbolizing the eyes of God: they "were looking down at me with scorn and impatience." (pp. 76–77)
After his almost total self-effacement, Marco step by step finds confidence in himself and life again. The people around him, his friend Zimmer, his love Kitty, his mentor Effing help him cope with his personal instability, and they consciously support Marco in his gradual psychic recovery. His sexual experiences, his love, his willingness to take over greater responsibilities – e.g. in the everyday duties of the couple's common household – are signs of an initiation completed and a new role accepted. The experience of loss, however, keeps haunting him. Marco loses his love, his hoped-for child and father-

hood, and later on also his new-found father. He relapses into a crisis which has parallels to his first one. In Chicago, he buries his father in a grave which was planned to be his own. He then stays in a hotel called Eden Rock Motel. Before he leaves his room he looks round at it: "If accommodations are provided in hell, I said to myself, this is what they would look like." (p. 293) In a fit of aggression he destroys the room from top to bottom. Here again Marco is depicted as a person struggling against his surroundings, trying to achieve a more mature stage of life. He runs away, taking his father's car and heading out west to Nebraska and further on to Colorado and Utah.

> "I understood that chance had taken me in the right direction. Without stopping to think about it, I had been following the road to the west, and now that I was on my way, I suddenly felt calmer, more in control of myself." (p. 294)

Stationed in Bluff, he makes all kinds of excursions in an attempt to find his grandfather's cave. He feels quite happy out there in the wilderness and, like his grandfather some 54 years before him, enjoys the solitude. When his car and money is stolen, he has hit bottom again.

> "I was like someone who had been struck by lightning. I thundered inside myself, I wept, I howled like a madman, but then, little by little, the anger seemed to burn itself out, and I settled into the rhythm of my steps. I went through one pair of boots after another. By the end of the first month, I gradually began talking to people again." (p. 297)

Marco has walked himself out of his second crisis to be a social being again.

> "Once I reached the end of the continent, I felt that some important question would be resolved for me. I had no idea what that question was, but the answer had already been formed in my steps, and I had only to keep walking to know that I had left myself behind, that I was no longer the person I had once been." (ibid.)

The fact that he has come to the end of his journey on January 6th, the Christian day of epiphany or 'revelation', hints at the significance of this event as a 'personal revelation' for Marco.
The process of self-discovery, his quest for identity seems to be completed. Moreover, after his painful journey to the West and to the Pacific the rising moon seems to create order, peace and harmony in his life – almost as it did for the Indians in Blakelock's painting. We do not learn what the center of his new-found identity really is. We also do not know if his greater maturity

protects him from relapsing into personal crises. But with the painful experiences of his remarkable journey, his confrontation with love and death, and the full knowledge about his origin, we get the impression that Marco Fogg has finally grown up. We presume that he is stable enough to bear the pressures of life and take up social responsibility – even in the East.
This second part of Marco's journey of initiation is typically American. Similar to many literary and western heroes Marco escapes from society and civilization, which really seems to be hell and not Eden for him, and moves into the vast American wilderness to encounter solitude and the remains of primitive American culture. His experiences in the West, the close contact with the American scenery and the physical efforts to be able to cross the rest of the continent on foot renew in him his spiritual powers and social abilities. There is a parallel between the United States which grew to maturity after the many treks had reached the Pacific and the frontier had vanished, and Marco, who after his solitary march through that same area reaches his destination. He is recreating the frontier spirit and at the same time he pushes himself to the limit.

Style

The choice of language and style in *Moon Palace* corresponds to the specific form of the narrative perspective. With the exception of Effing's monologue (Chapter IV) and the dialogues, the voice of the novel is Marco's. The conscious choice of a retrospective, older narrator, assuming that Marco Stanley Fogg is almost 40 years old when he writes down the story of his life between 18 and 25, allows Auster to employ a demanding style. The broad, creative choice of vocabulary adds richness and precision to the novel. One way to achieve this is Auster's effective use of adjectives:

> "For the first time since I had known him, Effing seemed absent, disengaged from the things around him, almost tranquil" (p. 197)
> "I had never slept during the day before, and all my old hiding places suddenly seemed precarious, exposed, useless without the protection of night. I kept walking north, hoping I would find something before I collapsed. The fever was mounting inside me, and a stuporous exhaustion seemed to be eating up portions of my brain." (p. 75)

Here, the various reasons for the uselessness of Marco's hideouts are given by adjectives, whereas the force of the fever is admirably expressed by metaphorical language. Strong, creative images are used throughout the novel:

> "[…] the furious, hell-bent energy of the toddlers who stormed and squealed around me […]." (p. 97)
> "It was a miniature pocket of life in the midst of overpowering barrenness." (p. 166)
> "The view from the cliff was immense, encompassing untold miles of terrain […]." (pp. 167)
> "His [Barber's] body was a dungeon." (p. 235)

Another example is Barber's emotional outbreak at Emily's grave. Barber's stammering utterances are characterized as follows:

> "The words tumbled out of him in a spasm of breathlessness, an onrush of grief that splintered into fragments as soon as it touched the air." (p. 284)

Baseball fan Auster is sure to use this game as a source of metaphorical meaning. Marco finds refuge in Central Park, his new 'home', near the 'Home' plate of a softball pitch. Marco explicitly employs the extended baseball metaphor to explain how he found the courage to take up contact again:

> "As Uncle Victor had once told me long ago, a conversation is like having a catch with someone. A good partner tosses the ball directly into your glove, making it almost impossible for you to miss it; when he is on the receiving end, he catches everything sent his way, even the most errant and incompetent throws. That's what Kitty did. She kept lobbing the ball straight into the pocket of my glove, and when I threw the ball back to her, she hauled in everything that was even remotely in her area: jumping up to spear balls that soared above her head, diving nimbly to her left or right, charging in to make, tumbling, shoestring catches. More than that, her skill was such that she always made me feel that I had made those bad throws on purpose, as if my only object had been to make the game more amusing. She made me seem better than I was, and that strengthened my confidence, which in turn helped to make my throws less difficult for her to handle. In other words, I started talking to her rather than to myself, and the pleasure of it was greater than anything I had experienced in a long time." (pp. 97–98)

Auster's sentence structures are quite varied and fluent, giving the prose a propelling force: "For three or four days in a row he had me read him pornographic novels (which were stashed away in a cabinet below the bookcase), but even those books failed to excite him to say to any noticeable degree" (pp. 196–197): adverbial phrase of time – main clause with infinitive without *to* – non-defining relative clause – main clause coordinated by *but*. Thus it becomes especially clear in the reflective passages that the style in *Moon Palace* is that of a highly educated narrator, a middle-aged university man who presents his story as a young man on a fairly high level of language and thought.

Themes – Motifs – Symbols

1. Journeys into the unknown: Columbus, Cyrano de Bergerac, Neil Armstrong

Marco Fogg is fascinated by journeys that take the form of travel into the unknown and amount to the discovery of new worlds. Columbus and his discovery of America which was really "a failure to reach China" (p. 40) are often reflected upon in the novel. Moreover, Auster obviously enjoys placing actions in a Columbian landscape: e.g. Columbia University (Marco, Zimmer, Barber), the "Columbia area" (e.g. p. 100), and Columbus Circle (e.g.: "Just north of Columbus Circle [...] an improbable occurrence took place. [...] I suddenly looked down and saw a ten-dollar bill lying at my feet", pp. 57–58). At the four hundredth anniversary of Columbus's discovery of America there is the Columbian Exposition in Chicago and young Effing can admire Tesla's exhibit of electrical tricks; this pavilion was called the "Egg of Columbus" (p. 142).
Marco considers himself to be an expert on moon travel – more in fiction than in fact – and he likes showing off his special knowledge.

> "Men had been going to the moon for hundreds of years, I said, perhaps even thousands [...]. I showered them [the ballet students at Zimmer's former apartment] with a history of moon lore, replete with references to Lucian, Godwin, and others." (p. 45)

Marco is especially fond of the life story of Cyrano de Bergerac (the fictional hero in Roland's play with the extremely long nose). According to Marco, Cyrano wrote a book about his moon travel in 1649 and presents there the most improbable details about life on the moon (p. 46). When Marco reads his father's books, he is, of course, attracted by Sol Barber's study on Thomas Harriot, who, as Barber maintains, was the first man to look at the moon through a telescope. Harriot beat Galileo by a few months. To assure us that Sol Barber is another moon fan, Marco tells us later in the novel that Barber is working on a longer book about Thomas Harriot (pp. 191–192).
In spite of his fondness of moon travels, Marco is a very distant and critical observer of Neil Armstrong's moon landing. He feels that something mythological has been destroyed. Armstrong plants a flag "in the eye of what once had been the goddess of love and lunacy. Radiant Diana, I thought, image of all that is dark within us." (p. 39) Marco thinks that man has lost his proper

course and Adam has his second fall: "[...] since the day he was expelled from Paradise, Adam had never been this far from home." (ibid.)

When Marco has to read out books to Effing, the first group of books deal with the question of travel. Marco, the born traveller, can in this way learn manifold versions of journeys into the unknown. So there is the journey of a legendary Saint Brendan who, in the fifth century, sailed from Ireland across the Atlantic to found the mythical kingdom of Prester John. Furthermore, there is, of course, the story of Columbus, the report on the Lewis and Clark expedition and a number of captivity stories – "firsthand accounts written by white settlers who had been abducted by Indians." (p. 113) Thus, Effing establishes himself as the teacher in Marco's journey, the story of his life.

Journeys into the unknown constitute the main leitmotif of the novel. Almost all male characters travel west, not knowing where their journey will really take them: the painters Moran and Blakelock, Effing the painter, Barber on his quest for his father's cave, Uncle Victor the itinerant musician ending up in Idaho, and finally Marco on his "pilgrimage" (p. 58) through New York and his lonely journey to the West and California.

2. Disappearance of Virgin (Indian) America

Blakelock's painting represents an American idyll to Marco. It is the world of harmony between man and nature, heaven and earth, it is the world "the Indians had inhabited before the white men came to destroy it." (p. 140) With the white men came people like the Gresham brothers, who had a negative influence on the native Americans. George Ugly Mouth can be seen as a representative of the process of degeneration. In our time, the old world of the West has vanished: Lake Powell has flooded the whole area in which Effing was able to enjoy the wilderness many years before.

3. The quest for the father

While Effing revolts against his father as a "fucking tycoon" (p. 147), and is glad to inherit his millions after his father's death and thus to become the richest painter in the world, his son and grandson are raised without fathers. Solomon Barber tries to create an image of his father by writing a booklet for the exhibition of his father's paintings and by writing a novel (*Kepler's Blood*) in which he gives literary expression to his fatherless childhood and his quest for his father. Marco has been completely left in the dark about his father. The absence of his father is part of Marco's identity. His male role model is

Uncle Victor, and it is therefore no wonder that he loses orientation after Uncle Victor's unexpected death. His employment with Effing sets into motion a painful process in which Marco gets to know his father and loses him again soon after. Marco, the narrator of this book, is so preoccupied with the gradual revelation of his true identity that his love for Kitty assumes only secondary importance. If the reader wonders why the quest for the father is such an important theme, he or she might find an answer in Auster's biography (see "Autobiographical Elements", pp. 78–79 in this study aid, and "The Author and his Times", pp. 5–12).

4. Self-abandonment

After Uncle Victor's death, Marco decides that the thing to do "was nothing: my action would consist of a militant refusal to take any action at all." (p. 28) He therefore does not take any action when his money gradually dwindles, when his books and 'furniture' disappear step by step and when, in spite of a very frugal life, he cannot prevent himself from being evicted.

> "I could follow the progress of my own dismemberment. Piece by piece, I could watch myself disappear." (p. 32)

It was clear to Marco that the development of his life pointed to self-destruction ("total eclipse", p. 28), but he felt a dark fascination which came from the simplicity of this plan to simply give in to his personal defeat.

> "This was nihilism to the level of an aesthetic proposition. I would turn my life into a work of art [...]." (ibid.)

This reasoning reminds us of Bartleby, the protagonist in Herman Melville's tale *Bartleby the Scrivener* (1853), who lives out his plan of total refusal up to bitter self-destruction, and of Oscar Wilde's Dorian Gray, whose downfall is regarded by Lord Wooten as a work of art, as a classical tragedy. Marco's life of hunger, deprivation and minimalist existence in his room and in Central Park are seen by him as an experiment to find out what will happen to mind and body in such a situation. He must recognize that this leads to unnatural introspection and egocentricity, ending in madness and ruined health.

5. Chance – coincidence

The action of *Moon Palace* is full of the strangest coincidences, so that Marco's story sometimes seems almost fantastic. Marco's relationship to Kitty Wu is established by a chance meeting at Zimmer's former apartment and they meet only because of the fact that both are wearing the same T-shirt that day. Marco's rescue in the vastness of New York and of Central Park by Kitty Wu and Zimmer is no less than a wonder. When Marco applies for a job, it is his own grandfather who gives him work and shelter. The novel also abounds in missed chances. Uncle Victor and Solomon Barber, who tries to find out more about Emily, have had extremely close encounters. Only trivial coincidences prevent Marco from meeting his father at a much earlier point in time. A similarly trivial coincidence allows Kitty to see through Barber's plan to arrange a meeting of reconciliation so that – from her point of view – she can avoid meeting Marco just in time.
Auster often introduces further action with the phrases "as luck would have it" (p. 171) or "as chance would have it" (p. 143). Furthermore, the novel presents many coincidences giving additional significance to the events in question. Marco gets 1492 books from Uncle Victor; the figure alludes to the journey of Columbus and may indicate that Marco is on a similar kind of journey to finally reach his destination. Effing dies on exactly the same day that he predicts. To Effing, this occurrence would have been proof of his personal philosophy. He thinks that you can control your destiny; it is up to you to bring order into your life and if you are consistent enough all will happen according to plan. He does not want to take any chances, and therefore carefully prepares everything he does with great circumspection and stubbornness. This view is based on an eccentric philosophical belief of the connectedness of matter and the electricity of thoughts. Effing maintains that he caused the New York blackout of 1965 by his own will and Marco replies:

> "It could have been a coincidence."
> "There are no coincidences. That word is used only by ignorant people. [...]
> If they're strong enough, a man's thoughts can change the world around him."
> (p. 108)

But Marco is not the master of the universe but its victim. His world is ruled by constant change and coincidence with the ever-changing moon as its main force. In his life, there is "One coincidence after another [...]. The universe seems to be filled with them." (p. 232) Chance, coincidence, change and disorder paradoxically seem to be the only reliable powers that create some kind of order.

> "Heraclitus had been resurrected from his dung heap, and what he had to show us was the simplest of truths: reality was a yo-yo, change was the only constant." (p. 69)

One day Marco reads Tesla's autobiography and comes across a sentence that he found in his fortune cookie almost a year before: "The sun is the past, the earth is the present, the moon is the future." Marco is deeply puzzled by this coincidence and tries to grasp the machinations of fate.

> "Had some worker in a Chinese fortune cookie factory been reading Tesla's book? It seemed implausible, and yet even if he had, why was I the person at our table who had chosen the cookie with that particular message in it? [...] I dropped my essay on Tesla and began exploring the question of coincidences, but I never got very far with it. It was too difficult a subject for me to handle, and in the end I put it to the side, telling myself that I would return to it at some later date. As chance would have it, I never did." (p. 229)

6. The moon

Marco, the narrator, refers to the moon in several contexts, he uses it in many varied combinations, and in some passages he comments on its qualities in great depth. The moon certainly assumes symbolic meaning, but it is impossible to define it clearly. As soon as you think that you have grasped the symbolic meaning of the moon in *Moon Palace*, there comes another passage in which this does not fit at all and you have to start anew. The meanings of the moon are as changeable as the moon itself.

> "Every now and then I would [...] watch the Moon Palace sign. Even that was enjoyable, and it always seemed to generate a series of interesting thoughts. Those thoughts are somewhat obscure to me now – clusters of wild associations, a rambling circuit of reveries – but at the time I felt they were terribly significant. Perhaps the word *moon* had changed for me after I saw men wandering on its surface. Perhaps I was struck by the coincidence of having met a man named Neil Armstrong in Boise, Idaho, and then watching a man by the same name fly off into outer space. [...] the words *Moon Palace* began to haunt my mind with all the mystery and fascination of an oracle." (pp. 39–40)

The moon and its palace arouse Marco's imagination, but it also confuses him ("why does the American West look so much like the landscape of the moon?", pp. 40) The action of the novel makes him feel moon-struck and

leads him towards lunacy (cf. *luna*, the Latin word for "moon"). But precisely in these phases of near madness the moon extends its benevolent powers to Marco. The two O's of the Moon Palace are compared to God's eyes which follow him critically and tell Marco that he is on a dangerous road. And at the end of the novel, it is the moon and "radiant Diana" – as it has been called before – which rises over the hills to bring light to the darkness of his life. In Blakelock's paintings, the moon and its light shine on scenes of peace and harmony between man and nature. To Marco it seems that it is the moon that creates this harmony (pp. 138–139). Marco sees the moon travel of the American astronauts as a violation of Goddess Diana's realm. In contrast to the American President, who celebrates this feat of human ingenuity, Marco considers the moon landing to be an action standing for man's hybris to infringe on God's sphere: "[…] since the day he was expelled from Paradise, Adam had never been this far from home." (p. 39)
The ambiguity in the moon's meaning is also alluded to in the cryptic oracle of the fortune cookie (p. 101) and Tesla's autobiography (p. 229): "The sun is the past, the earth is the present, the moon is the future." It seems to be the moon, i.e. constant change, that determines Marco's future and his cycles of life. He carries the little paper slip with the oracle with him for nine months to find it again in his wallet when a new cycle of life has begun for him.
In spite of its obscure and ambiguous quality, the moon can give direction in life: "A man can't know where he is on the earth except in relation to the moon or a star." (p. 154) For Marco this is also true on a symbolical level.

7. Art, language and reality

As in a traditional "Bildungsroman", Marco is introduced into the various spheres of life including the world of art and literature. Effing encourages Marco to look at paintings as well as to read and even to write books.

> "The things he said to me, the books he chose for me to read […] were these part of an elaborate and obscure plan […]? At times I felt that he was trying to pass on some mysterious and arcane knowledge to me […]. This was Effing as crackpot spiritual guide, as an eccentric master struggling to initiate me into the secrets of the world." (p. 111)

Effing is surprised when he learns that Marco does not know Blakelock.

> "Don't you know anything about painting? I thought you were supposed to be educated. What the hell did they teach you in that fancy college of yours, Mr. Smart Ass?" (p. 135)

When Marco answers “Not much” (p. 135), Effing undertakes to teach Marco to see, describe and assess paintings, taking Ralph Albert Blakelock’s *Moonlight* as an example. Marco learns that the deeper meaning of a painting lies beneath its surface. After a careful and very methodical observation of *Moonlight*, Marco sees that there is more to it than meets the eye: “It was not a landscape, it was a memorial, a death song for a vanished world.” (p. 140) Marco has clearly learned how art can give form to reality and express truth about it.
For Effing, art and painting is a means of survival during his isolation in the Rocky Mountains. At the same time, the experience of the gigantic landscape and its immense emptiness leave a deep impression on him and shape his artistic concepts. He develops a new and more mature approach to painting.

> “He was working for himself now, no longer burdened by the threat of other people’s opinions, and that alone was enough to produce a fundamental change in how he approached his art. For the first time in his life, he stopped worrying about his results, and as a consequence the terms ‘success’ and ‘failure’ had suddenly lost their meaning for him. The true purpose of art was not to create beautiful objects, he discovered. It was a method of understanding, a way of penetrating the world and finding one’s place in it […].” (p. 169)

For Marco, reading Uncle Victor’s 1492 books is more a matter of coming to terms with his feeling of loss than trying to read them consciously for their relevant meaning and aesthetic enjoyment. Only in Effing’s service is he compelled to dig deeper and to read more purposefully the books given to him by his employer. As Effing also expects him to give a convincing assessment of what he has read, he is forced to read carefully. To fulfill his task of writing Effing’s obituary, i.e. his life story, Marco learns how to write three different forms of text referring to the same topic but with a different audience in mind and different intentions. After listening to Effing, Marco is required to give form to the words, and thus he finds out how by writing he can bring order to a seemingly chaotic sequence of events. Marco puts his new skills to use later when he writes the story of his own life in book form. When he starts doing so, it is as though he is starting his life anew: “That was a long time ago, of course, but I remember those days well, I remember them as the beginning of my life.” (p. 7) Marco describes the close interrelationship between writing, literature and life: “If life was a story […] and each man was the author of his own story, then I was making it up as I went along.” (p. 49) Books are a means to recreate and to come to terms with reality and with one’s life. Even if they are as fanciful as Sol Barber’s *Kepler’s*

Blood, they serve this function. But can language really grasp and render reality or will it always fall short of it? Marco works hard on Effing's demands to describe everyday objects like a lamp-post or clouds in the western sky or even Blakelock's painting, but he mostly fails. He learns that the human tendency to generalize is inadequate, that only close observation and concrete description, short and clear sentences are able to evoke a realistic picture of the world for a blind person.

> "To get what he wanted, Effing should have hired Flaubert to push him around the streets – but even Flaubert worked slowly, sometimes laboring for hours just to get a single sentence right." (p. 123)

Here, Auster reflects upon the question whether literature can express reality and he conveys his pessimistic postmodern view.

> "A fire hydrant, a taxi cab, a rush of steam pouring up from the pavement – they were deeply familiar to me, and I felt I knew them by heart. But that did not take into account the mutability of those things, the way they changed according to the force and angle of light, the way their aspect could be altered by what was happening around them [...]." (p. 124)

On the other hand, it is only language – though limited – that makes conscious perception possible.

> "What do you see? And if you see, how do you put it into words? The world enters us through our eyes, but we cannot make sense of it until it descends into our mouths." (ibid.)

8. Telling names

Auster likes to use both open and hidden word plays about the names of his characters. He makes them philosophize on the special meanings of their names' components. Together with Uncle Victor, Marco finds all kinds of references and associations in his name. Above all, they see Marco as the born traveller. *Marco* stands for *Marco Polo*, *Stanley* for the man who found Livingstone, *Fogg* for Phileas Fogg (*Around the World in 80 Days*) and for Fogelman from which it is derived. Marco imagines that one of his ancestors must have been a bird flying through fog (p. 9) and this seems to be true for his life, too. He is more often in fog than he would like. As an adolescent Marco has a special liking for the "literary" abbreviation of M. S. (manuscript) for his first names. This abbreviation is meant to be an allusion to Marco's youth being

only the 'manuscript' of his life story, which was changed considerably by the later events starting in the time the narrator describes as the "beginning of his life" (p. 7) – "Every man is the author of his own life [...]. The book you are writing is not yet finished", as Uncle Victor puts it (p. 13). Thomas Effing carefully chooses his pseudonym: *Thomas* from the name of the original cave dweller Tom, Thomas Moran and the biblical doubting Thomas; out of contempt for himself and his life's failure, he transforms the association of *fucking Thomas* into *f-ing* and modifies it to *Effing* for his surname (pp. 182). Solomon Barber makes an intellectual theory about his Christian name's short form Sol, which in Latin means both "sun" and "ground". So as a young man he felt flattered to think that "he alone was able to encompass all the contradictions of the universe." (pp. 246–247)
Auster's humorous play with names can be found in *Barber* who is completely bald, in *Victor* who is more a loser than a winner and in *Zimmer* who is Marco's roommate and who, as Marco's friend, has the function of giving him a room.

9. The magical figure "nine"

It is striking that Auster often uses a nine-month period to organize a certain development of action; these actions take the form of cycles and allude to new beginnings and rebirth:

- "[...] for the first nine months I [Marco] lived in a dormitory." (p. 7)
- Marco carries the slip of paper with the oracle of the fortune cookie along with for nine months (p. 102).
- "Within nine months he [Effing] was rich again" (p. 183).
- "It took him [Effing] nine months to recover " (p. 186).
- "For the next eight or nine months, I lived [...] [in a state that came close to] human paradise." (p. 224)

Uncle Victor's life philosophy is that everything works out fine in the end because everything connects:

> "The nine circles. The nine planets. The nine innings. Our nine lives. Just think of it. The correspondences are infinite." (p. 14)

To him, the figure "nine" rules both our cosmos and our life on earth and gives order to it. His somewhat naïve belief does not turn out to be true for his life is also determined by unexpected change and coincidence. At its lowest point, it meets rather an abrupt end.

10. Penance / atonement

Both Marco and Effing have a strong longing to atone for their antisocial and immoral behavior and feel relieved if punishment is dealt out to them by fate. Effing dutifully accepts his severe injury as the form of penance he has to pay for the murders he committed and the kind of life he led in California. His eccentric idea of handing out money to complete strangers in the streets of New York is a form of delayed atonement. Marco is also overcome by the feeling of repentance and in his first turnabout after his rescue decides to lead a life like a saint. Similarly, Solomon Barber's attitude after his affair with Marco's mother is characterized by the idea of atonement. In *Moon Palace*, Auster seems to draw these ideas less from Christianity or Judaism than from his favorite book *Crime and Punishment* by Dostoyevsky. It is certainly the case that the ideas of wrongdoing and penance are strong motives which determine the behavior of the major characters in *Moon Palace*.

Characters

A Survey

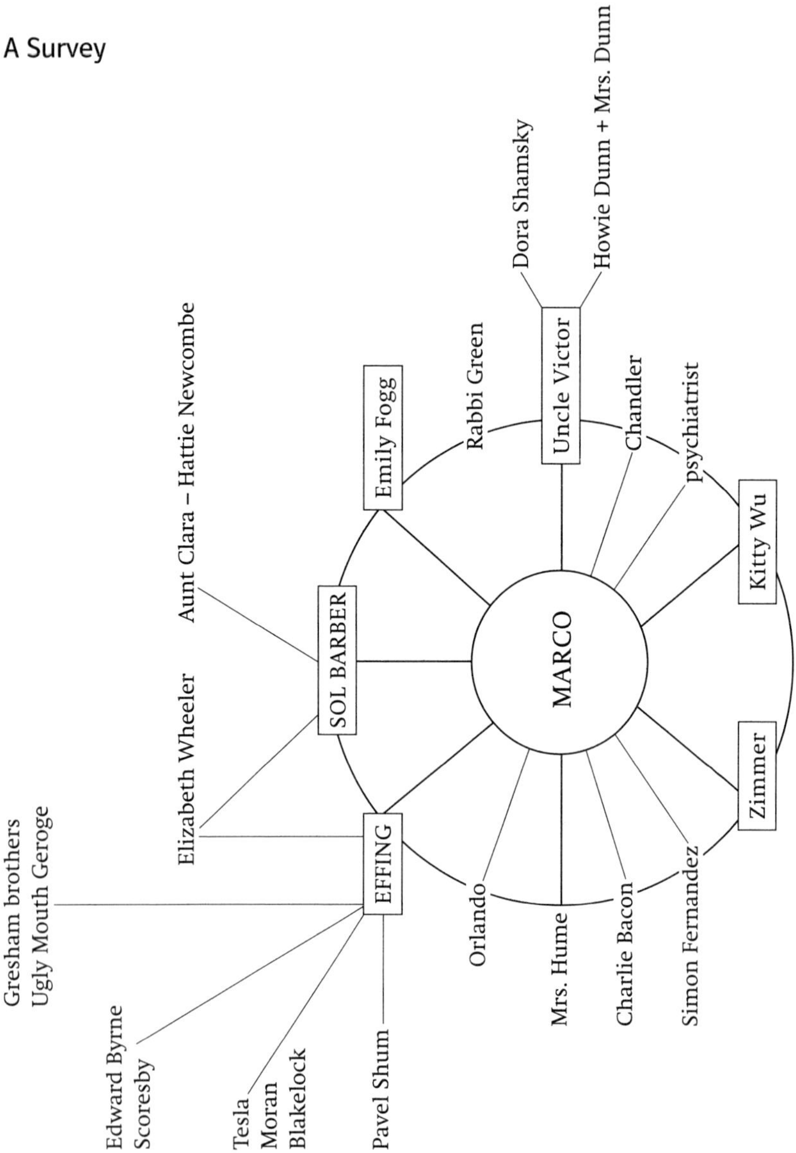

Marco

Marco Stanley Fogg is born in Chicago in 1947. He is the son of Emily Fogg and Sol Barber, Emily's history professor. Marco grows up in a single-parent family, unaware of his father's identity, and after his mother's fatal accident in Boston, the eleven-year-old boy becomes an orphan. He is well looked after by Uncle Victor, his mother's brother. Marco had a very close relationship to his mother and he often likes to remember the fine times they had together, for instance sitting in the cinema, eating popcorn and holding hands. There is not a single trace of a father in his home – not a photo, not even a name, and so young Marco imagines him to be a space traveller who has passed into the forth dimension and cannot find his way back. Once he is called "poor Emmie's love child" by an acquaintance of Uncle Victor's. Marco is troubled by this, but he does not really know what is meant. When he asks Uncle Victor, he is given the Solomonic answer: "All children are love children, [...] but only the best ones are ever called that." (p. 11) Marco misses his mother and apparently suffers from this loss, but his guardian uncle soon wins his love and adoration. Marco enjoys being with him, going to the cinema, playing all kinds of games and watching and talking about baseball. Marco's receptive mind is much influenced by Uncle Victor's stories and eccentric ideas. Victor helps him to form an idea of his personal identity by interpreting his name, although here he is only partially successful. Marco has a feeling "for the infinite fragility" (p. 13) of his name. Nevertheless, Marco is fascinated by the idea that all the elements of his name indicate travel and mobility: Marco and Fogg remind him of Marco Polo and Phileas Fogg, Stanley is the name of the man who found Livingstone. Marco's grandfather Fogelman, a European Jew, was given the truncated form of Fog for his name by some "half-literate" American immigration officials at Ellis Island when he entered the country. Later the second g was added.

> "A bird flying through fog. I used to think, a giant bird flying across the ocean, not stopping until it reached America." (p. 9)

The variability of his identity takes on further forms when Marco adopts the habit of calling himself "M. S." (short for *manuscript*); he thus tries to prevent his classmates from turning his names around in all kinds of fashion to ridicule him. He is Phileas to his uncle, he is M. S. to his classmates at college and Kitty sometimes calls him Foggy, a name that suits his unclear mind very well. Marco is rarely used. Zimmer and Effing just calls him Fogg. Marco's near obsession with his name reflects his attempts at discovering his true identity. Like his two Barber forefathers (Solomon and Julian Barber), Marco is an eccentric person, a fact that he is aware of and even cultivates.

> "Looking back on it now, I realize what a curious figure I must have cut: gaunt, disheveled, intense, a young man clearly out of step with the rest of the world. But the fact was that I had no desire to fit in." (p. 22)

He enjoys playing the role of the outsider whose intellect and genius set him apart from his peers. He does not mind his fellow students seeing him as an "oddball" (ibid.), it pleases him to behave like this:

> "[…] I would spend whole nights in bars smoking and drinking as though I meant to kill myself, quoting verses from minor sixteenth-century poets, making obscure references in Latin to medieval philosophers […]." (ibid.)

Marco likes to wear the tweed suit he inherited from Uncle Victor to emphasize his nonconformity. Undoubtedly, this is a demonstrative rejection of the uniform blue jeans, the Hippie look and the anti-bourgeois revolt of his generation. When the suit is worn out, he turns to the other extreme and buys the cheapest, but most durable clothes he can get: work boots, blue jeans, flannel shirts, and a second-hand leather jacket from an army store. Judging from his wide and even sometimes exotic knowledge of literature and history, the reader is led to assume that at school and college Marco has pursued his studies with great interest and extreme energy. He reads widely – working his way through all 1492 of Uncle Victor's books in a fairly short span of time – and is by all standards an unusually learned young man. He is given to dreams and fantasies, and, like Uncle Victor, he tends to create extraordinary theories about otherwise banal events. From his apartment, Marco can see the neon sign of a Chinese restaurant which reads MOON PALACE:

> "[…] the force with which those words assaulted me drowned out every practical reference and association. They were magic letters, and they hung there in the darkness like a message from the sky itself." (p. 24)

Marco is raised in the Jewish faith; so he has his bar mitzvah in Chicago at the age of thirteen. The ceremony is conducted by Rabbi Green. He has his mother buried in the Jewish cemetery of Westlawn, Chicago, and, later, he even arranges for his father, a gentile (i.e. a non-Jew), to be buried there, too. It seems to be more religious conviction than eccentricity that leads Marco to persuade 'his' 70-year-old Rabbi Green to conduct the funeral and to recite only Hebrew prayers. When Marco visits his mother's grave, he puts a stone on the plate, instinctively following the Jewish custom of remembering dead people. Marco's language quite naturally resumes biblical imagery of the Old Testament comparing his personal rescue to the history of the Israelites: "I had been lost in the desert, and then, out of the blue, I had found my Canaan, my promised land" (p. 224).

Marco's background seems to predestine him not to follow a well-ordered path to adult life. As the times are in turmoil (Vietnam War, student revolt, moon landing), so is Marco's life, and there is no political or personal orientation he can follow.

> "My own story stands in the rubble of those days, and unless this fact is understood, none of it will make sense." (pp. 32–33)

Marco half-heartedly goes along with the student movement, he is a member of left-wing student organizations, and once he even gets arrested during a riot on Columbia campus. He does not see any sense in going to Vietnam as a soldier and one of his main fears is to be drafted.

Uncle Victor's death robs him of his only personal support at a time when his money is dwindling, and his health and mind suffer from his lack of food and his increasing isolation. Verbally he praises Zimmer as his best friend and the only person he can count on, but he does not turn to him when he feels that his despair has taken hold of him and that his life is heading towards an existential crisis. In his tendency to mystify the events of his life, he sees himself as a lonely probationer of a purely personal experiment:

> "[…] I didn't want anyone to interfere with the course I had set for myself. […] I walled myself up in the delirium of my project […]." (p. 34)

His project is nihilistic, namely not to do anything:

> "I decided that the thing I should do was nothing: my action would consist of a militant refusal to take any action at all." (p. 28)

He wants to find out what in detail will happen when step by step even the bare necessities of life disappear and everything turns to zero. The fatal end is part of his scheme: "Total eclipse. […] The moon would block the sun, and at that point I would vanish." (ibid.) In part this experiment is the quest for a minimal self and the age-old fight of mind over matter.

Marco, the widely-read literature student, is aware of the many literary heroes who have trodden the same path in their lives. Although he does not refer to these examples by name, it is obvious that he refers to Thoreau (p. 34), to Melville's Bartleby (the symbol of passive refusal, p. 27) and, in a more vague form, to Knut Hamsun, Kafka and Oscar Wilde. During his period of isolation in his apartment and in Central Park, his mind and his body gradually deteriorate. He loses weight, the power of concentration and the power of clear thought. He is given to developing theories which justify his behavior. He likes to think, for example, that his life as a bum in the park is a conscious protest against the overflowing abundance of American capitalism. The spectacular series of defeats of the Chicago Cubs of that year confirm his newly won philosophical truth about life and the world: causality no longer rules the universe; the ruling principles are change and reversal:

> "[…] down was up, the last was the first, the end was the beginning. Heraclitus had been resurrected from his dung heap, and what he had to show us was the simplest of truths: reality was a yo-yo, change was the only constant." (p. 69)

After his rescue, Marco first goes to the other extreme. He detests his former egotism and self-involvement and fervently wants to make good for the pain he has inflicted on his fellow human beings through his behavior. He wants to become a model of responsibility and helpfulness. In an almost religious fanaticism he intends to atone for his sins and do penance (p. 73). However, these endeavors are mainly abstract. The reader might expect that his further life centers round Kitty; her wishes and her happiness could well give meaning to his life. Instead, he enters upon a long and painful quest for a father. He is preoccupied with Effing's and Barber's life stories. His relationship to Kitty, however important it may be for his mental well-being, is marginal and unimportant compared to his gradually unfolding family background. When Kitty is pregnant, he is incapable of understanding her point of view. His wish to become a father and to establish a secure family unit is dominated by egocentric motives. With respect to Zimmer, his second savior, he shows complete and cold-hearted neglect for the rest of his life.

Marco's attitude towards Effing and Barber is determined by a love-hate relationship, with love and understanding winning the upper hand in the end in each case. His unconscious feelings of familial bonds make him overcome his initial dislike of the men. After much inner conflict, Marco accepts his identity as Effing's grandchild and Barber's son. When closely watching the change in Barber's face in the hospital, Marco recognizes something familiar. Some time later he is overcome by a shock of recognition when all of a sudden he realizes that he has the same eyes as Barber. "I realized that I was looking at myself […]." (p. 289)

After his father's death, Marco tries to return to Kitty to find a sure haven to be able to cope with the confusing events of finding and losing a father within a few weeks. But it is only his great personal despair that makes him call Kitty. If he had called her earlier because of his concern for her, there might have been hope for the renewal of a well-balanced relationship. However, Kitty senses that Marco is still preoccupied with himself and his crisis and rejects his pleas. At last Marco goes the way of many an American hero, including his grandfather. He goes West, crossing the American continent in the hope that this journey will create a new person and a new beginning.

Julian Barber alias Thomas Effing

The man with two identities is a very complex character. There are manifold facets to his personality; taken together they leave an ambivalent impression on the reader.

At the same time, the reader must be careful when forming a picture of him because we cannot be sure if the information we have is reliable. Effing enjoys leaving things unclear. The matter of his blindness remains a mystery even to Marco. Perhaps he only wants to play the role of the old blind 'seer' who can even predict the date of his death.

The reader may be amused by Effing's eccentricities (the show of distributing money in the streets), he or she may respect his extremely strong will and pragmatic attitude in difficult situations, but Effing's egocentrism, his ruthlessness and his tyranny over the people in his household tend to arouse negative feelings in the reader. His sharp wit and his sarcasm are expressed in a language which may be refreshing for the reader, but rather insulting for the people around him. Marco, who has to put up with Effing's whims and moods, sees the two sides of his character:

> "He was a monster, but at the same time he had it in him to be a good man, a man I could even bring myself to admire." (p. 120)

During his expedition to the West, for instance, Effing shows responsibility and genuine comradeship towards his young companion, Byrne, but he also displays great ruthlessness towards the Gresham brothers. Furthermore, the ever suspicious and sarcastic Effing develops an unusual sympathy and friendship to his companion, Pavel Shum; they stay loyal to each other for thirty years, which, for the changeable Effing, is a very long time. On the other hand, towards his son, Sol Barber, whom he has never seen, Effing shows neglect and no sense of parental duty. Towards Marco, Effing adopts the role of a mentor. The way in which he prepares Marco for the job of writing his life story gives Marco the impression that Effing pursues a hidden

strategy. He is instructed in the quality of art, he is required to sharpen his verbal skills, to use language to describe reality and he becomes acquainted with Effing's critical view of technological progress.
Although he is a frail little man, Effing likes challenges and goes through life with irrepressible vitality. He remains optimistic despite his personal setbacks and masters his problems with courage. Effing boasts of his sexual vitality and freely reveals his disappointment in his wife's frigidity.
In his view, there are no coincidences in life. He thinks that everything in the world is connected by electricity and is therefore calculable and to be manipulated. Life is consequently a matter of willpower for Effing. He even maintains that he caused the New York blackout by sheer willpower (p. 104).
Effing regards himself as one of the great American artists (p. 131). This assessment is not supported by facts or further information. As to his style, we only learn that he did not attempt to copy the styles of his great idols, Thomas Moran and Ralph Albert Blakelock. We can, therefore, only assume that his paintings were "more modern". His reputation concerns him – he is completely dissatisfied with the obituary that was published after his presumed death in the West; therefore, he has decided to write an obituary of his own in order to present a 'true' picture of his art and his life to be published after his death.

Solomon Barber

Solomon Barber has a stigma from birth: he has a gigantic body. While his mother suffers from mental derangement, Solomon's trouble is a physical one, namely obesity. Born a huge baby, he grows up to be an enormous man. Solomon reaches his full adult height by the age of 15 (six foot two/ three = 1.90 m) and puts on a considerable amount of weight. In his adolescent years he tries to keep his weight below 250 pounds (113 kg); he tries to keep to diets, but after university his weight increases to 290 pounds (132 kg). His dismissal from college plunges him into a personal crisis, and he becomes increasingly obese ("he ate his way to the brink of oblivion", p. 237), adding another thirty-seven pounds to his weight (so he weighs almost 150 kg) – the contrast to his anorexic son could not be greater. Barber uses his obesity as a protective shield, "to shut himself off from the world" (ibid.).
Solomon Barber is an intellectual and extremely knowledgeable man. In reaction to the mockery and ridicule he is constantly confronted with because of his size, he turns to reading. From early on, books become his refuge from people and from self-preoccupied thoughts. With his books he is able to for-

get his abnormality. It is therefore not surprising that he graduates top in his class and even achieves previously unheard-of grades and test scores. Like Marco some 29 years later, he goes to Columbia University. He studies history, and his thesis on Bishop Berkely and the Indians wins the American Studies Award. Despite offers from renowned Eastern universities, he decides to go to Ohio to teach history at a second-rate college. He is very successful at every college he goes to, mainly because of his academic brilliance and his lively teaching style. He works hard, produces articles and books, goes to conferences, gives interesting lectures, and devotes much of his time to his students, with whom he is always very popular. His exceptional appearance and his reputation as the fattest history professor soon make him well-known on each campus he goes to. In addition, he cultivates his eccentricity: he continually smokes long cigars and, as he has become completely bald, he takes to wearing hats – a different one each day, it seems; soon he is widely known as the "Man Who Wore Hats" (p. 238).

Solomon Barber's publications demonstrate his strong interest in the early colonial history of America. The Indians and the primeval American wilderness often feature in his books, and in this respect Solomon Barber echoes his father's interests. He might have been influenced by the Blakelock paintings which he could often admire when he was in his family's dining room. He vividly remembers the special quality of the moonlight scenes depicting Indian life.

The servants of his family call him Solly and later Sol.

> "The Elizabethan poets taught him that this was an old word for 'sun', and not long after that he discovered it was also the French word for 'ground'. It intrigued him that he could be both the sun and the earth at the same time, and for several years he took it to mean that he alone was able to encompass all the contradictions of the universe." (pp. 246–247)

As a boy, he writes a novel based on his father's disappearance called *Kepler's Blood*. "Part Western and part science fiction" (p. 249), the story is highly improbable; but its main theme, unfolded in many variations, is the quest for the father and the son. Of the three major characters in *Moon Palace* Solomon Barber is probably hit hardest by the breakdown of his family. He has never met his father and is kept in the dark about him in his formative years, he has fathered a son but does not know about it until shortly before his death. Emily was the only woman Barber ever loved. There is no question that this both intelligent and warmhearted man takes a great liking to his son, a feeling he must hide till the whole story comes out in an uncontrollable way.

In his will, Solomon Barber leaves his family's large Long Island house to his Aunt Clara. He sees some kind of irony in this as Aunt Clara, a former vaudeville girl who married Elizabeth Wheeler's brother and who was looked down upon by the rich Wheeler and Barber families, is now their heir. The irony becomes complete and assumes an almost political dimension when Sol Barber dictates that afterAunt Clara's death the house goes to their black servant Hattie Newcombe. Moreover, this decision is further proof of Barber's liberal and unconventional mind.

Uncle Victor

Uncle Victor – the brother of Marco's mother – is "a spindly, beak-nosed bachelor" of forty-three who earns his living as a clarinetist (p. 11). Although he lacks ambition, Uncle Victor must have been a good musician because for some time he is a member of the famous Cleveland Orchestra. Like all of the Foggs, he is characterized by a certain aimlessness in life. He does not settle down, but is constantly on the move. Because of a thoughtless joke, he has to leave the renowned Cleveland Orchestra. He then plays in smaller combos: the Moonlight Moods and later the Moon Men. In order to earn a sufficient living, he also gives clarinet lessons to beginners. His last job is selling encyclopedias.
Uncle Victor is given to dreams, his mind restlessly shifting from one thing to another. He is interested in baseball and in all kinds of sport. His rich imagination and creativity allow him to invent playful activities for his nephew Marco. Uncle Victor carries out his guardianship for Marco in a responsible way, but he does not exercise adult authority over Marco. He forms a relationship based on sympathy, love and friendship. Marco loves his uncle's easygoing lifestyle, his humor and his generosity. Uncle Victor is also quite openminded, likes movies and is fairly well-read, with more than 1000 books.

Zimmer

Although Marco sees Zimmer as his best friend, the narrator treats him like a flat character. In many ways, Zimmer is a contrastive figure to Marco. He is open to others, very helpful, he pursues his studies with great energy and determination and manages to overcome personal difficulties successfully. He is not a dropout and does not seem to be involved in the turmoil of the times. Zimmer is smaller than Marco (p. 82), he is "a wiry person with curly black hair" (p. 93). The metal-rimmed glasses and his beard make him look "something like a young rabbi." (ibid.) Zimmer studies Comparative Literature, he is an expert on French literature, and his chief concern in his young life is writing poetry. In his academic studies, Zimmer is conscientious and systematic and Marco thinks that "of all the undergraduates I had known at Columbia, he was the most brilliant" (ibid.). Nevertheless, Marco's eccentricities seem to make him the dominant partner in their friendship. Zimmer grew up in the New Jersey suburbs where he met his girlfriend Anna Bloom.

With great helpfulness, Zimmer (a telling name: it is his task to give Marco 'room') offers Marco shelter and food in his apartment. He goes to great trouble to help his friend towards a fast physical and mental recovery. Without fuss, Zimmer makes considerable sacrifices, and lets Marco have his large room and his bed while he sleeps on the floor in an adjoining small room.

For the reader, it is disappointing to see how such an intense friendship ends with no apparent reason. While Marco is preoccupied with wheeling Effing through New York, neither Marco nor Zimmer make any effort to stay in contact. In a very laconic style Marco informs us:

> "I said my good-byes to Zimmer that night [...] and traveled uptown to Effing's apartment. As chance would have it, I did not see Zimmer again for thirteen years. Circumstances pulled us apart [...]." (p. 109)

By sheer accident they meet again in 1982 in the streets of Lower Manhattan. The narrator informs us that Zimmer is married, has two boys, that he is a university teacher and has written a lengthy study of French film, but not a single poem. Although this chance meeting induces the narrator to write down his present narrative, it is in itself a cold and unemotional anticlimax of a once warm friendship. Maybe here again, Zimmer and his well-ordered bourgeois life is only used as a contrast to Marco's own complex development. In this context, it is interesting to note that we do not learn what becomes of Marco after 1971. The narrator, although presenting his story from a point in the eighties, does not inform the reader about what happened to him after January 6th, 1972.

Kitty Wu

Kitty, born in 1950 in Taiwan, is the daughter of a Chinese Kuomintang general and his second concubine. At the age of fourteen, Kitty is sent to Fielding Academy, a boarding school in Massachusetts. Later, with her father's small inheritance, she goes to the ballet school of Juilliard, N.Y. Her career as a dancer is of central importance to her. She is a warmhearted young woman and is always in good spirits. When Marco first meets her at a party, he is immediately attracted by her beauty and openness. She is small and behaves very naturally; she wears no makeup and no bra, but there are silver bracelets on both wrists and a beaded Navaho band around her head. In a very spontaneous way Kitty – partly playfully but partly seriously – kisses Marco good-bye when he leaves the party:

> "'I'm your sister, after all, and I'm not going to let you leave without kissing me good-bye.' […] Kitty stood on her toes, put her hand on the back of my neck, and kissed me – very tenderly, I felt, almost with compassion." (p. 47)

Kitty obviously falls in love with Marco at first sight. There is an immediate mutual understanding. They seem to be very much alike, being almost two parts of a whole. Chance has it that they are both wearing the same T-shirt and are humorously seen as twins by the party guests. Marco senses this fundamental similarity when he observes that both had a similar kind of childhood ("Orphans in the storm, that kind of thing […] I suppose there are certain resemblances", p. 92).
When Marco finally declares his love to her, Kitty honestly admits that she has been waiting a long time for this. With great naturalness and without any embarrassment, Kitty seems to enjoy the physical love which now develops in their relationship. She always displays good humor and gets along well with Marco and all other people. She dresses in extraordinary and attractive clothes, accentuating the shape of her body.
When Marco and Kitty set up their small household in a loft and Kitty has some weeks off, she insists on taking up a job to be an equal partner in their relationship. She does not want to live on Marco's money (p. 226).
Kitty is very ambitious. She is intent on finishing her training as a dancer and on becoming a ballerina. So, when she becomes pregnant, she takes the choice to have an abortion. She suffers from this decision, which destroys their relationship, but she is firm in setting the priority on her career, and has the abortion carried out. In spite of their conflict over the abortion, she appeals to Marco on her knees begging him not to leave her as she still loves him very much. In Marco's absence, she misses him even though he gives no sign of life for quite some time. When Marco finally tries get into touch with Kitty, it is too late. Kitty has apparently entered into a new relationship.
The narrator does not give Marco's and Kitty's relationship the significance many readers might expect. Marco seems to be preoccupied with the quest for his father and does not see that his love for Kitty could be an answer to his personal problems. The fact that Kitty is a Chinese girl has to be seen

as an important aspect within Marco's journey and, in this way, within the framework of the novel. Standing at the Pacific, Marco thinks he is at the end of the world, except that beyond the emptiness there is China. It only needs the imaginative power of Uncle Victor to bring all this into harmonious context.

> "Had Uncle Victor lived to meet her [Kitty], I'm sure he would have appreciated the fact that Marco, in his own small way, had at last set foot in China." (p. 14)

Other Female Characters

In *Moon Palace,* Auster makes intensive use of stereotypes to depict its female characters. Mrs. Hume, for instance, is presented as the robust good spirit every household needs. With her gigantic breasts, her never-ending energy, her unbelievable patience, she is presented as a stock character that you can find in many novels and movies. The same kind of stereotyping is employed in the case of Aunt Clara the vaudeville dancer (she likes her sherry and takes life easy), and with Elizabeth Wheeler (the sexual reserve of the upper class and also the depiction of her madness). Even Emily Fogg, Marco's mother, remains one-dimensional. After the affair with her professor, she withdraws and bravely copes with her fate on her own. Marco's memory of her and their time together is positive but restricted to a few rather typical things. It is really astonishing that Auster does not give greater prominence to the role of women, e.g. in the case of Kitty.

Minor Characters

There is a series of minor figures who are depicted as flat characters. Nevertheless, many of these are represented with precision and love for detail. Some of them make interesting observations and make the reader see how strangely Marco behaves and how serious his derangement is. The caretaker Fernandez, for instance, vividly expresses the view of the common man – he shakes his head about the behavior of a university student:

> "You've got some place here, my friend. If you don't mind me saying so, it reminds me of a coffin." (p. 52)
> "[...] you just sit around on your ass all day. Like some chimp in the zoo, you know what I mean?" (p. 53)

Similarly, the army psychologist shows his professional concern at the mental state of the young man, and Rabbi Green, who is the victim of Marco's eccentricity, is unable to really help him and advises him to consult a doctor. In this way, the reader sees how serious people assess Marco's confusion. With Mrs. Hume's brother, Auster presents the cliché figure of the madman who, in moral terms, is completely sane. The revolt of Charlie Bacon against human self-destruction is somewhat naïve, but it is deeply felt and moving. The Gresham brothers and George Ugly Mouth can be seen as characters who represent the degeneration of the 'Old West'. Then there is Chandler, the heartless bookseller: he is a man without emotions who is only interested in books for their material value and who completely ignores Marco as person. Mr. and Mrs. Dunn, however, are portrayed as warmhearted people who readily help others in distress, i.e. Marco after Uncle Victor's burial. And finally Auster presents Orlando as the embodiment of the 'lunatic spirit' in the novel. Besides Hattie Newcombe, he is the only black character in *Moon Palace* and plays the role of the funny eccentric. On a cloudless spring evening, Orlando walks or dances through the streets of New York. He is holding up an opened umbrella which no longer has its protective covering. He invites Marco and Effing to get out of the imaginary rain and take shelter under his deconstructed umbrella.

> "Our host's name was Orlando, and he was a gifted comedian, tiptoeing nimb -ly around imaginary puddles [...]. This was imagination in its purest form: the act of bringing nonexistent things to life, of persuading others to accept a world that was not really there." (pp. 206–207)

This leaves us wondering if Auster sees his role as a writer exactly in this same make-belief project.

Autobiographical Elements

Both Paul Auster and his hero Marco are born in 1947, indicating that the author wants the reader to see the existing parallels between fiction and reality: Both Paul and Marco are fond of baseball and have the same favorite clubs, both attend Columbia University, both want to avoid the draft for Vietnam, both try to keep their heads above water by translating French texts into English, both suffer from extreme hunger at one time in their lives. Beyond these concrete similarities they also have one theme in common: the search for one's father. Auster, who craved for a caring father in his youth (see "The Author and his Times", pp. 5–12), here creates a hero 'without a father'. The variations on the theme of losing and finding a father in *Moon Palace* are presumably developed out of Auster's personal feeling of loss. His father's death seems to have been the crucial event that triggered off his creativity in the field of fiction.

A further parallel can be found in the fact that Auster has his narrator, Marco, write his story in 1986, which is probably the time when Auster started to write *Moon Palace*. Yet apart from the mentioned parallelisms the life stories of the author and his protagonist are very different. *Moon Palace* displays Auster's great imaginative creativity in the formation of the eccentric and exotic characters of Thomas Effing and Solomon Barber who definitely have nothing in common with Auster's father and grandfather. The writer uses biographical data freely so that Marco's friend Zimmer has distinctive features of Auster himself. It is Zimmer and not Marco who comes from New Jersey and it is Zimmer and not Marco who writes poetry – as Auster did as a student. It is also Zimmer who studies Comparative Literature at Columbia University – as Auster did. When Marco speaks about Zimmer you might feel that Auster speaks about his student times:

> "Zimmer's chief concern in life was writing poetry, and he spent long, hard hours at it, laboring over each word as if the fate of the world hung in the balance – which is surely the only sensible way to go about it. In many respects Zimmer's poems resembled his body: compact, tightly sprung, inhibited. His ideas were so densely woven together that it was often difficult to make sense of them. Still, I admired the strangeness of the poems and the flintlike quality of their language." (p. 94)

The various places or apartments in Manhattan (Zimmer's and Marco's accommodations) are probably recreated from Auster's personal life as a student there. Effing's love of France, his early stay there as a student remind us of Auster's own youth. Here, too, Auster seems to speak about his early life and about Effing's at the same time:

> "He was not looking for paradise, he merely wanted a country where he would not be bored. England was out of the question (he found the English despicable), and while the French were not much better, he had fond memories of the year he had spent in Paris as a young man. Italy also tempted him, but the fact that French was the one foreign language he could speak Solomon Barber Emily Fogg with any fluency tipped the balance to France. At least he would eat well there and have good wines to drink." (pp. 187–188)

Factual Allusions and References

Young Marco is an extremely erudite student who acquires a lot of further knowledge over the years in which we accompany him through the novel. In this context *Moon Palace* can rightly be called a 'Bildungsroman' in a different sense. For a reader coming from a non-American background, much of the novel's allusions to everyday America is not easy to follow, particularly as the novel starts over 30 years ago. The reader has to work hard and use the help of annotations to understand the many allusions and references to the political, cultural, and literary history of the USA and beyond. The allusions provide the reader with a kaleidoscope of both classical and trivial knowledge which could well be the corpus of a quiz. Indeed, Marco and Barber do play that quiz.

> "Later on, when the sun began to go down, we spent more than an hour enumerating our preferences in every area of life we could think of: our favorite novels, our favorite foods, our favorite ballplayers. We must have come up with more than a hundred categories, an entire index of personal tastes. I said Roberto Clemente, Barber said Al Kaline. I said *Don Quixote,* Barber said *Tom Jones*. We both preferred Schubert over Schumann, but Barber had a weakness for Brahms, which I did not. On the other hand, he found Couperin dull, whereas I could never get enough of *Les Barricades Mystérieuses*. He said Tolstoy, I said Dostoyevsky. He said *Bleak House*, I said *Our Mutual Friend*." (pp. 282–283)

It is, however, not necessary for the reader to be familiar with all these books, authors, composers and so on, for Auster uses this abundance of references to confuse the reader, as a device to make his own writing more interesting and cryptic and to keep the reader hooked. Thus, he also uses many ideas from European and American literature and, above all, from popular fiction and from films.

Appendix

Marco Stanley Fogg's Genealogy

Old Barber
(millionaire)
d. 1906

Elizabeth Wheeler – – – – – – **Julian Barber/**
Thomas Effing
1883–1970

Solomon Barber – – – – – – – – – – – Emily Fogg
1917–1971 1929–1958

M. S. Fogg
b. 1947

Bibliography

Works by Paul Auster

Fiction

The New York Trilogy (1987) (*City of Glass*, 1985; *Ghosts*, 1986; *The Locked Room*, 1986)
In the Country of Last Things (1987)
Moon Palace (1989)
The Music of Chance (1990)
Leviathan (1992)
Mr. Vertigo (1994)
Timbuktu (1999)
The Book of Illusions (2002)
Oracle Night (2004)
The Brooklyn Follies (2005)
Travels in the Scriptorium (2007)

Poetry

Ground Work: Selected Poems and Essays 1970–1979 (1980)
Disapperances: Selected Poems (1988)

Screenplays

The Music of Chance (1993)
Smoke (1995)
Blue in the Face (1995)
Lulu on the Bridge (1998)

Essays and Autobiographical Texts

The Invention of Solitude (1982)
The Art of Hunger (1992)
The Red Notebook (1995)
Hand to Mouth (1997)
"Why Write?" in: *The New Yorker*, December 25, 1995 and January 1, 1996.

Secondary Sources

Moon Palace Book Reviews

Birkerts, Sven, "Postmodern Picaresque, *Moon Palace* by Paul Auster", in: *The New Republic*, March 3, 1989, pp. 36–40.

Kakutani, Michiko, "A Picaresque Search for Father and for Self", in: *The New York Times*, March 7, 1989.

Kornblatt, Joyce Reiser, "The Remarkable Journey of Marco Stanley Fogg", in: *The New York Times Book Review*, March 19, 1989, pp. 8–9.

Criticism

Addy, Andrew, "Narrating the Self: Story-Telling as Personal Myth-Making in Paul Auster's *Moon Palace*", in: QWERTY. *Arts, Littératures et Civilisations du Monde Anglophone* 6 (1996) pp. 153–161.

Birkerts, Sven, "Paul Auster", in: *Essays on Fiction*, New York: William Morrow, 1992.

Bloom, Harold (ed.), *Paul Auster*, Philadelphia: Chelsea House, 2004.

Klepper, Martin, *Pynchon, Auster, Delillo: Die amerikanische Postmoderne zwischen Spiel und Rekonstruktion*, Frankfurt/New York: Lang, 1995.

Reinhart, Werner, *Pikareske Romane der 80er-Jahre (Acker, Auster, Boyle, Irving, Kennedy, Pynchon)*, Tübingen: Narr, 2001.

Seidl, Christian, "Regeneration through Creativity – The Frontier in Paul Auster's *Moon Palace*", www.fu-berlin.de/phin/phin31/p31t5.htm (Philosophie im Netz 31/2005)

Springer, Carsten, *Crises: The Works of Paul Auster*, Frankfurt/New York: Lang, 2001.

Weisenburger, Steven, "Inside Moon Palace", in: Dennis Barone (ed.), *Beyond the Red Notebook:* Essays on Paul Auster, Philadelphia: University of Pennsylvania Press, 1995, pp. 29–142.

Interview

Begley, Adam, "Case of the Brooklyn Symbolist", in: *The New York Times Magazine*, August 30, 1992, pp. 41, 52–54.

TV Portraits

"Paul Auster Confidential", by Gerard de Constance and Guy Seligman, Arte TV, Germany, October 27, 1998.

"Paul Auster – Mein Leben," by V. Grandits and J. Krauss, ZDF, 2006.

The Critics

Moon Palace and the myth of the American West

"[...] Mr. Auster invents an aging rich man named Thomas Effing, who hires Marco Fogg as his companion and becomes Marco's wacky spiritual guide, tormentor and benefactor. Effing tells his own story at length (Marco writes it down as the old man dictates) so that his narrative functions as a kind of tale within the tale, its meanings opening up to us as Marco's own saga progresses. Effing claims to have been a somewhat famous painter who, after a series of mishaps, tragedies and debacles, makes a journey on foot through the transforming landscape of the American Southwest – 'the land is too big out there, and after a while it starts to swallow you up' – and survives, half mad, in a cave he fills with paintings. 'He untaught himself the rules he had learned, trusting in the landscape as an equal partner, voluntarily abandoning his intentions to the assaults of chance, of spontaneity, the onrush of brute particulars. He was no longer afraid of the emptiness around him.'
In this way Mr. Auster works the mythology of the American West into *Moon Palace,* its beauty and violence and Indian mysticism a counterpoint to the gritty New York terrain the rest of the novel details. And it is no surprise that the final leg of Marco Fogg's odyssey takes our hero himself to that primal landscape. But not before he discovers the shocking truth about Effing's long-lost son, Solomon Barber, an obese itinerant history professor (and of course his scholarly focus is the American West) who has also written a kind of futuristic pulp western, which we hear about at some length. In a moment of rage, Marco attacks Solomon Barber, his dear friend seemingly turned traitor, and the larger-than-life father figure falls, fatally injured, into a freshly dug double grave, feet away from Marco's own beloved mother's grave, which Marco has taken Barber to visit on their journey west. [...]

Moon Palace (the title refers to a Chinese restaurant in New York) is held together by unlikely coincidences. All the characters are eccentrics who border on caricature, yet their struggles are heartfelt and complex. The plot of the novel is so unbelievable, its narrator often has trouble being convinced by it himself. And the motifs are extremely familiar: the beleaguered orphan, the missing father, the doomed romance, the squandered fortune, the totemic power of the West, the journey as initiation. Yet the story is, finally, so goodhearted and hopeful, so verbally exuberant, that its obvious architecture, its shameless borrowings, may be forgivable. I wondered: was this an early novel that Paul Auster reworked, in hopes of a wider audience, after his years as an experimental and elusive stylist? Or is *Moon Palace* a determined retreat from the growing darkness of his own prior work, of which he writes in his moving memoir about fatherhood, 'The Invention of Solitude': 'In that the world is monstrous. In that it seems to offer no hope of a future, A. looks at his son and realizes he must not allow himself to despair. There is this responsibility for a young life, and in that he has brought this life into being, he must not despair.' [...]"

Joyce Reiser Kornblatt, "The Remarkable Journey of Marco Stanley Fogg," in: *The New York Times Book Review,* March 19, 1989, p. 8. –

Inheritance: *Moon Palace*

'The solution to the identity problem in *Moon Palace* is strikingly different from that presented in the preceding novel, *In the Country of Last Things.* While Anna Blume establishes a (new) identity by living with friends, with a partner, or in an 'artificial family', *Moon Palace* emphasizes that only the connection with the male family line can provide points of reference and orientation; this patriarchal idea of inheritance is made to appear as the only 'authority' that can lead the protagonist to finding his identity. Fogg's life is part of this genealogical principle which dominates, in this novel, over all other forms of contact among people.

The 'cycles of repetition', which structure the novel's action, elevate the inheritance principle to the status of omnipotent fate. [...] The story thematizes the protagonist's disorientation in a 'reality' which appears as complex and, at first, incomprehensible (because of the lack of relatives as figures for identification). But ambivalence and plurality, illustrating the postmodern living conditions, are pushed into the background in favor of the 'metanarrative' of family relations and inheritance. The journey reaches its destiny: in contrast to many destructive postmodern texts, in which [...] 'writing (becomes) an endless journey' of 'always searching, always asking, and never receiving an answer', the written journey in *Moon Palace* reaches its destination when answers are indeed found.

With regard to form, *Moon Palace*, like Auster's preceding novels, shows his use of postmodern textual practices. The numerous stories and episodes contained within the novel are all intratextually linked and connected by an intricate web of related motifs. Furthermore, these stories belong to or partake of a great number of different genres, thus intertextualizing the individual in a typically postmodern way. Effing's story mixes travel account and adventure novel, 'fact' and fiction, and is supposed to serve as an obituary; Barber's life is made to resemble an aborted romance, while his book *Kepler's Blood* draws heavily on science fiction. The aspect of mixing genres in *Moon Palace* is reminiscent of Mikhail Bakhtin's theory of 'carnivalized' literature and definition of the picaresque novel. *Moon Palace* can be seen both as 'carnivalized' text and as a picaresque novel, and also as a *bildungsroman*. In my opinion it is this last term which is the most fitting one for the identity development shown in this text. The life stories of Effing and Barber function as instructions for the development of Fogg's identity, which is completed at the end. Even a superficial comparison with classic *bildungsromans* such as J. W. Goethe's *Wilhelm Meisters Lehrjahre* (1795), Novalis' *Heinrich von Ofterdingen* (1802), or modern examples of the genre such as Ralph Ellison's *Invisible Man* (1954), reveals numerous parallels to *Moon Palace* in terms of structure and contents.

As in *The New York Trilogy*, Auster again makes use of a number of autobiographical details in this novel. But in contrast to the novels of the *Trilogy*, the author follows a different aim in *Moon Palace*: personal experience is cast into a fictional mold. The textual strategy is less one of intertextuality or the mixing of ontological levels than the attempt of a 'portrait of the author as a young man' (who, significantly enough, wrote the first drafts of the novel around 1969–72, the period of the novel's action). As Auster concedes, '*Moon Palace* … sounds more like an autobiography than any of my other novels.'

Chronologically and thematically, the novel occupies a central position within Auster's oeuvre. Its narrative style appears more traditional and at the same time more 'typical' for Auster than the preceding novels. After the deconstructive postmodern textual games of the *Trilogy* and the allegorical escape from postmodernity in *In the Country of Last Things*, *Moon Palace* is a book in which the postmodern reconstruction shows many points of overlap with modern literature. By asserting the traditional structural model of the *bildungsroman*, as well as through further parallels to modern novels like Knut Hamsum's *Hunger* and Thomas Mann's *Zauberberg*, *Moon Palace*, more than any preceding work by Auster, distances itself from the conventions of deconstructive postmodern literature. As a postmodern *bildungsroman*, the novel testifies to Auster's movement towards a reconstructive postmodern mode."

Carsten Springer, *Crises: The Works of Paul Auster*, Frankfurt / New York: Lang, 2001 (American Culture, Vol. 1), pp. 152–154.

Auster's world: hunger and the absent father

"[...] The theme of the absent father is recurrent in Auster's story. His first prose fiction *The Invention of Solitude*, written after his father's death, was an attempt to fill in the void left by his absence. Auster is painfully aware of the absurdity of his task, of the impossibility of entering another's solitude: the man would let you get as far as he wants you to come. Auster's father is the epitome of the postmodern character: 'an impenetrable space in the block of time'. (*The Invention of Solitude*, p. 7) The figure of the father looms in the background of Auster's fiction. [...]

Moon Palace offers another version of late origin. Narrated in concentrated circles, it evolves around the three generations of complete strangers who belong to the same family. Chance encounters bring unforeseen changes to their lives: at the centre of this dysfunctional family universe is the comical overweight figure of Sol Barber who, as the story turns out, is Marco's father. For Aristotle these moments of recognition [as a shift from ignorance to awareness, see p. 36 in *Poetics*] between members of close family bear not only intense drama but bring about 'peripety' [reversal, a shift of what is being undertaken to the opposite [see p. 36 in *Poetics*] of the dramatic action. For Auster it is just another story which boils down to a series of missed chances. The pieces of jigsaw puzzle are there from the beginning but nobody bothers to fit the together. All the movements in the novel are cyclical; no sooner does Marco Fogg finish one cycle of his life than he begins another. until he ends up literally at the end of the world beyond which there is nothing except emptiness. As the Moon finds its way in the darkness of the sky, Marco ponders about the new beginning. The Moon has a feminine, repetitive nature. It is the object of desire, the urge to capture it is seen as a symbol of progress. It also, as Byrne said in the novel, helps define man's position on Earth. As Marco wanders around New York like forsaken Adam whose life becomes total chaos an decay, he overhears the words of the American president who greets the first steps on the Moon as the greatest in the history of humanity.

The theme of hunger is another important feature of Auster's story. Image of a hungry artist links him to Knut Hamsun and Kafka. It expresses the hunger of the artist for whom the writing has become a compulsion and matter of survival. It expresses Auster's idea of writing as compulsion and the obsession of the artist who must write in order to stay alive. The art becomes need, necessity and desire. Auster's essays on literature are published under the title The Art of Hunger. The artist who produces the art of hunger starves to create. [...]

Marco Fogg's anorexia on the border hand comes as a form of resistance. The protest against society is refined to the form of aesthetic nihilism, through radical refusal to do anything to help his position. He is certain that once the money runs out he is going to starve and possibly die but still he resolves to do nothing as a form of protest to the world. He decides to become living proof that the something rotten in the land of plenty. Similarly in a short story by Kafka, [Kafka, Franz, 'Fasting Showman' in *Wedding Preparations in the Country and Other Stories*, Penguin, 1978] the aesthetics of hunger receives most meticulous elaboration. The story is called 'The Fasting Showman' and is centred upon the figure of a hunger artist who is sitting in a cage performing his art of fasting. His eagerness to show off his skill prompts him to stretch out his arms through the bars so people might feel how thin they are. He takes painstaking measures to make sure that his art of fasting is genuine, although he is watched day and night by the guards he even whistles in their presence to let the know that he is not helping himself to some nourishment in secret. He fasts in order to be admired, however the public gradually loses its taste for his art and he fies in the straw of his forgotten cage. [...]"

Dragana Nikolic, "Paul Auster's Postmodernist Fiction: Deconstructing Aristotle's 'Poetics'" [Thesis], www.bluecricket.com/auster/articles/Aristotle.html

Model Questions and Answers

I Comprehension

1. Auster starts his novel with Marco (aged 22) watching the Moon Landing of July 20th 1969 in a bar. By way of various flashbacks Auster establishes Marco's life as a boy and young student. Briefly sum up the information given about his family, his childhood, his school and university years.
2. Explain briefly how the the life stories of three seemingly complete strangers are intervowen in the course of the action.
3. Work out chronological lists of the life stories of J. Barber / Th. Effing, Solomon Barber and Marco Fogg.

II Analysis and Interpretation

1. Describe how Marco is characterized in the first three chapters of the novel.
2. What does the fact that Marco plays about with the wider meanings of his various names (Marco, Stanley, Fogg, MS) express for his character?
3. What does Marco completely throw off-course in his second student year? Describe his then following life of gradual self-abondonment or, as he sees it, his experiment of "mind over matter".
4. Forced to give up his isolated life in the narrowness and emptiness of his student's flat Marco retreats to Central Park. Explain/discuss what he means when he says: "There is no question that the park did me a world of good."
5. Who is to blame for the breaking-up of the love relationship between Marco and Kitty? Why do later attempts at reconciliation fail?
6. Nearly all female characters are depicted as "flat characters". Analyze how Auster makes use of stereotypes in dealing with women (e.g. Marco's mother, Mrs. Hume, Elizabeth Wheeler, Dora Shamsky). Discuss if Kitty's portrayal is an exception to this.
7. Give a brief description of the scene depicted in Blakelock's painting *Moonlight*. What is the deeper significance of the painting in Marco's view?
8. Discuss the relevance of the moon for the meaning of the novel.
9. Life as a journey and references to journeys of various kinds make up for for one of the main leitmotifs of the novel. With travellers such as Marco Polo, Columbus, Stanley, Armstrong and the novel's characters, e.g. Effing, Solomon Barber, Uncle Victor and Marco in mind – what are the

various conditions and experiences of being a traveller? What – in particular – does the journey West mean to these characters?

10. In one way or another all three male major characters suffer from the "loss" or the absence of the father. Analyze how this fact affects their lives.
11. Why does Effing throw his money away to the public in New York City?
12. Chance and coincidences play a major role for the action of the novel. Discuss some of them. Marco comes to believe that chance may be the ruling force of man's life. Describe Effing's view of man and destiny.
13. Do you think that Marco's painful journey to find his identity and his initiation into the hard facts of adult life have been successfully completed, when after his long march he sees the moon rising over the Pacific at Laguna Beach? Explain your view.

III Text Production

1. **Letter to Kitty:** Having reached Laguna Beach on the Pacific Marco writes a letter to Kitty.
2. **Personal Comment:** Discuss Marco's aestheticism. Can life be taken as a work of art? Cf. the following statements: "Every man is the author of his own life" (p. 13, Uncle Victor); "If life was a story [...] and each man was the author of his own story, then I was making it up as I went along. I was working without a plot, writing each sentence as it came to me and refusing to think about the next" (p. 49, Marco); "I would turn my life into a work of art sacrificing myself to such exquisite paradoxes that every breath I took would teach me how to savor my own doom" (p. 28, Marco about his wilful path to doom).

IV Dealing with Literary Criticism

1. Explain J. R. Kornblatt's statements taken from the text "The Remarkable Journey of Marco Stanley Fogg," in: *The New York Times Book Review*, March 19, 1989 (see this study aid p. 84: "*Moon Palace* and the myth of the American West").
   - Thomas Effing becomes Marco's "spiritual guide, tormentor and benefactor."
   - The meaning of Effing's tale is "openening up to us as Marco's own saga progresses."
   - "Mr. Auster works the mythology of the American West into *Moon Palace*, its beauty and violence and Indian mysticism" as a counterpoint to the gritty New York terrain which the rest of the novel details.

2. What is Kornblatt's main focus in his interpretation of the action of the novel?

Material for Suggested Answers

I,1

Marco Fogg and his mother's family

- Marco's grandfather on his mother's side is a European Jewish immigrant named Fogelman; when he immigrates at the turn of the 19th century, a "half-literate" American immigration officer "americanized" this into "Fog" which he himself changes to "Fogg".
- Fogelman's/Fogg's daughter, Emily Fogg, is Marco's mother. As a history student at college she has a one-night love affair with her professor, Solomon Barber. They are caught in flagranti and Emily immediately leaves the college with unknown destination breaking off all contact to the professor. She masters the time of pregnancy on her own and gives birth to a son whom she calls Marco Stanley Fogg. In utmost discretion Emily does not give the smallest hint about the father neither to her son Marco nor to anybody, even not to her brother Victor. When Marco is eleven years old, Emily Fogg, who has earned her living at a textbook company Cambridge (Mass.), dies in a road accident in Boston. She is buried in Chicago in the same cemetery as her parents.
- After his mother's death Marco is taken care of by his mother's brother, Victor Fogg, a bachelor. Victor is a professional musician and is, like all the Foggs, a bit of a dreamer gifted with a rich imagination. Because of an insulting joke he has to leave the prestigious Cleveland Orchestra. This is the start of quite a turbulent life. However, Uncle Victor cares for his nephew with great empathy and good humor. He is more a friend than a father to Marco. He administers the insurance payment Marco received from Boston Transport in compensation for his mother's death. Victor sees to it that Marco succeeds at high school. At the age of eighteen Marco can start his freshman year at New York's Columbia University. In April 1967 when Marco has just finished his two undergraduate years Victor unexpectedly dies in Boise (Idaho) where he was on the way as an encyclopedia salesman.
- Marco Stanly Fogg is born in 1947 and is raised by his mother in a single parent family. They live in Boston and Cambridge. Marco, who has only a rather vague image of his mother, is told by her that his father died before he was born.
- After his mother's death (1958) the eleven-year-old Marco moves to Chicago to Uncle Victor who at that time is unmarried. They develop a very

close relationship, more the one of friends than that of father and son. They have common interests (baseball, inventing games, imaginary travels to fantastic lands) and Uncle Victor supports Marco by his presence whenever he plays baseball in the Little League. Marco's success at baseball gives him the much needed self-confidence and helps him "over some hurdles at school" (p. 14). After a while they move to Saint Paul and soon after that back to Chicago again which makes making friends difficult.

- When Marco is fourteen, Uncle Victor marries the capricious Dora Shamsky. The marriage turns out to be an unhappy one and Marco is sent to a boarding school in New Hampshire (Anselm's Academy for Boys). To pay for this some of the money determined for university fees is prematurely spent. In due time, namely after three years Marco graduates from the high school of Anselm's Academy.
- In 1965 at the age of eighteen Marco starts his freshman year at Columbia University (N.Y.C.), presumably majoring in English literature. As a freshman he is obliged to lodge in the College dormitory. He shares his room with David Zimmer who becomes his best friend.
- For his second year the eccentric Marco rents an apartment on West 112th Street to be on his own. From one of the rooms he can just look through a gap down onto Broadway and on the neon sign "Moon Palace" of a Chinese restaurant. Marco does not furnish his apartment, but packs it full with boxes which serve as makeshift tables and chairs. The boxes contain 1492 books which are given to him by Uncle Victor who after the failure of his marriage goes out West with a band.
- In April 1967 Uncle Victor unexpectedly dies and Marco who has just finished his undergraduate studies rapidly loses the ground under his feet and is finally thoroughly thrown off-course. His apathy and psychic depression prevent him from taking up his graduate studies. But to avoid the draft for Vietnam he decides to stay enrolled at Columbia University, even if this means that by and by the fees eat up his diminishing money reserves.
- For two years Marco lives an extremely austere and isolated life in his apartment. Book by book he reads through Uncle Victor's 1492 books and after having read a score of them sells these to get some money to buy food. On 20th July 1969, on the day of the moon landing, Marco sells the last portion of books. Life to him becomes an increasingly desperate affair. His attempts at contacting Zimmer fail and after a month he is evicted from his apartment. He is down and out in New York with no money and no person to turn to.

I,2

Son – grandfather – father

- The first part of the novel deals with Marco Fogg and his life from 1947 to 1969. The main action explicitly sets in with Marco's first year at Columbia University in the fall of 1965. By way of flashbacks embedded in the introductory passages of the exposition Marco presents his childhood and school years. As the first-person narrator Marco selects those facts he thinks relevant for his life's story. For the narration of the events of the proper action from 1965 onwards Marco does not adopt the unlimited perspective of looking back on his life from 1986. We follow the main stages of his internal crisis mainly from the simultaneous point of view of the suffering and staggering Marco. In great detail we get to know Marco's experiment of total rejection, of not doing anything. The reader sympathizes with this helpless orphan on his path to an obviously inevitable doom: his eviction from his apartment, his life in Central Park and his almost fatal illness. The story of his rescue, his recovery during the fall of 1969, his falling in love with Kitty concludes this first part wholly concentrating on Marco.
- From November 1st (1969) onward Marco is employed by Thomas Effing, an eccentric and handicapped old man, as a companion. Here Marco and the reader are told in lengthy sessions the eventful life story of a certain Julian Barber. As a young painter he leaves his wife to go on an expedition to the American West. He is involved in a story of murder and shoot-outs and is forced to live in a cave for some time. He manages to escape with some money and decides not to return home, but to adopt a new identity (Thomas Effing) and start a new life in the West. In San Francisco he gets rich in no time, is seriously injured one night, goes to live in Paris, returns to New York where he still lives at the time of the main action. Effing knows about the existence of his son Solomon Barber, but does not contact him. Neither Marco nor the reader can sense that this strange old man who sometimes not very reliably tells this remarkable story of his life (as the second part of the novel) is Marco's own grandfather.
- After Effing's death (on 12th May 1970) Marco fulfills his promise to contact Julian Barber's (i.e. Effing's) son Solomon Barber to hand over one of the obituaries. But they meet only as late as October 1970. In further contacts with this enormously obese, but very learned and quite pleasant history professor, Marco and the reader get to know Solomon's life story (part three of the novel). Solomon Barber knows from the very beginning of their contact that chance brought his son to him. The reader can conclude that there are father and son dealing with each other, whereas Marco is left in the dark about the real relationship between Professor Barber and his remarkable student Emily Fogg.

- Parallel with the presentation of parts of Solomon Barber's life Marco tells the reader about his love for Kitty, his great happiness in their common flat and the bitter story of their separation caused by the conflict over the abortion of their baby.
- In early summer 1971 Marco Fogg and Solomon Barber go on a journey West together (beginning of part four of the novel). At Emily's grave in Chicago Solomon Barber's tears reveal to Marco that Sol Barber was his mother's lover and that this "colossus" is his father. Sol Barber falls into an empty grave and is seriously injured; in long talks at the hospital Marco is informed by Sol Barber about the missing links in his life's story.
- On September 4th 1971 Solomon Barber dies and Marco has him buried next to his mother.
- Marco's attempt to win back Kitty fails. He sets out west towards to Utah finding the presumed cave of his grandfather Effing flooded by Lake Powell. His car is stolen and Marco continues his journey on foot. He reaches the Pacific on January 6th 1972.

I,3

Julian Barber

1883	Julian Barber is born.
1905/06	Julian's father dies and the painter Julian Barber inherits millions.
1912	Julian Barber marries Elizabeth Wheeler.
1916	Julian Barber leaves for his great expedition to the American West.
1916/17	Julian Barber's expedition fails; left alone he spends his time in a cave painting.
1917	Julian Barber goes to California and takes up a new identity as Thomas Effing.
1919	Thomas Effing suffers a serious injury after an attack and with the help of a companion moves to Paris.
1939	Effing returns to New York, fleeing from the Nazis.
1969	Effing hires Marco Fogg to be his companion and write his obituaries.
1970	May12^{th}: Effing dies.

Solomon Barber

1917	In January Elizabeth Wheeler gives birth to the huge boy Solomon.
1934	The extaordinarily gifted and intelligent student Solomon Barber writes a novel to cope with his fatherless youth.

1935	Solomon Barber attends Columbia University (N.Y.C.).
1939	Solomon's mother dies; he becomes a professor of history and teaches at various colleges in the Midwest.
1946	Solomon Barber has an affair with his student Emily Fogg who then cuts all contact with him although she is pregnant.
1947	Marco Fogg is born; Solomon Barber does not know about his having a son.
1970	In October Solomon Barber meets Marco Fogg and soon suspects that Marco is his and Emily's son.
1971	On September 4th Solomon Barber dies in Chicago.

Marco Fogg

1947	Marco Fogg is born; he spends his early childhood with his mother in Boston.
1959	Marco's mother is killed in a traffic accident.
1958–62	Marco lives with his uncle Victor in Chicago and some other places.
1962–65	Marco stays at a private boarding school in New Hampshire.
1965–66	Marco's freshman year at Columbia University; he lives with David Zimmer in the College dormitory.
1966	After his first year Marco decides to live on his own in an apartment at West 112th Street with a view of Broadway and the Chinese restaurant "Moon Palace".
1967	Towards the end of Marco's second university year Uncle Victor dies.
1967–69	Marco lives an isolated life in his apartment; he leaves university without graduation.
1969	In August Marco is evicted from his flat and stays in Central Park for 3 weeks; in September Kitty and David Zimmer save Marco's life. On November 1st Marco begins his service with Thomas Effing.
1970	On May 12th Thomas Effing dies; in June Marco and Kitty together move into a flat, in October Marco becomes acquainted with Solomon Barber.
1971	Kitty has become pregnant and has an abortion and they separate. In July Marco and Solomon Barber set out for the West. Solomon Barber dies in Chicago on September 4th. In October Marco starts on his three month's walk to the Pacific.
1972	On January 6th Marco watches the moon rise over the Pacific at Laguna Beach.

II,1

Marco Fogg – characterization

- In the first chapter the reader mainly has to rely on the first-person narrator Marco himself who presents his character as he perceives it from the retrospection of 1986. Later with the appearance of David Zimmer and Kitty the picture becomes less one-sided, as both friends do not refrain from criticizing Marco for his lack of confidence. His behavior in social contact situation like the house-warming party, the eviction scene and the army physical reveal his eccentric character and his disorder in soul and mind.
- Marco presents himself as a torn personality which oscillates between timidity and arrogance. He often displays the pretentious pose of the "sublime" intellectual showing off with his immense literary knowledge and academic superiority. At the same time he suffers from existential insecurity, a lack of self-confidence and inner fragility.
- In his identity crisis and as a young man who does not know who he really is he clings to Uncle Victor as his last support. During his undergraduate years he wears Uncle Victor's tweed suit as a badge of identity and as a second skin, that is to shield him from the blows of life. He derives pleasure from being seen as an odd fellow who stands apart from the mass: "if my fellow students pegged me as an oddball, that was not my problem" (p. 22).
- Marco's ongoing quest for his true self is elucidated by Marco himself when he plays about with the meanings and variations of personal names: Marco Polo, the first European **traveller** to visit China; Stanley, American journalist who goes on an **expedition** to find Dr. Livingston in Africa, Phileas Fogg (*Around the World in Eighty Days*); MS meaning manuscscript, something not finished, not perfect; Fogg derived from Fogelman (an allusion to being free like a bird, like a bird flying through fog); Foggy and Cyrano, favorite names used by Kitty. All these names express something vague, something that is always on the move to somewhere far away and they stand for Marco's character who has not yet found a firm center and his true self. Furthermore the taunting transformations of his name used by schoolmates leave him "with a feeling for the infinite fragility of my name" (p. 13).

II,2

The experiment of "mind over matter"

- After his mother's death Uncle Victor is the person Marco loves "most in the world" (p. 8).
- In fact he is the only person the orphan Marco can turn to and rely on. Marco sees him as his only "link to something larger than himself" (ibid.).
- Victor's sudden death robs Marco of his only emotional and personal support. The feeling of personal loss hits Marco hard. Feeling orphaned again he sees himself as the target of the inimical forces of fate.
- After the first intense grief is spent (p. 26), Marco out of a feeling of despair decides to accept his fate and to let fate decide about him. In total rejection of the demands of life he is determined to go a nihilistic way to "total eclipse": "I decided that the thing I should do was nothing: my action would consisit of a military refusal to take any action at all […] I would do nothing to thwart the inevitable […] the moon would block the sun, and at that point I would vanish" (p. 28).
- Thus for almost two years Marco's lethargy and rejection of life compell him to gradually do without most and even the barest things that are basic to the subsistance of life: Marco's quest for a "minimal life" make him run out of the necessary things of life, namely money, books, proper clothes, ink, electricity, toilet paper, soap, razor blades, candles, friends, means of communication, weight, clear perception of the world around; finally time would run out for him. The material, emotional and social basis of life diminishes and threatens to vanish.
- The funds for his university education dwindle faster than originally planned; in order to pay the fees and the rent Marco makes a little money by gradually selling Victor's books to a second-hand book store. He systematically economizes on food and his art of hunger just stops short of starvation. He continously loses weight which finally in August 1969 goes down to only 123 pounds: "I was trying to separate myself from my body" (p. 37) in order to see if mind can win over matter. In the end Marco is confronted with his mind drifting away; "there were periods when I simply lost track of myself". In acknowledging his defeat in his experiment Marco recalls Sir W. Raleigh's remark before his execution: "My brains are broken." (p. 50)

II,3

Central Park

- To be wholly down and out in the streets of New York is quite a new and demanding challenge to Marco. In his inner turmoil Marco's moods constantly change between joy and despair. One moment he feels confident that he can make it, but the next he realizes his state and is shocked about himself. He feels he has turned himself into a nothing and has thus failed Uncle Victor.
- In contrast to the socially controlled behavior in Manhattan, life in Central Park offers Marco shelter, privacy and freedom: "the majority of people who came in there acted as if they were on holiday. The same things that would have alarmed them in the streets were dismissed as casual amusements [...]. It was live and let live." (p. 64)
- In place of the self-imposed isolation of his flat, life in Central Park brings along social contacts both of pleasant and unpleasant kinds. Once he even accepts the invitation by a group of young people to join them in a game of baseball.
- Marco enjoys the park's solitude that protects him from the reqirements and demands reigning in the world outside; amidst the hub of a metropolis it represents home, a refuge and solitude to him.
- Many of Marco's positive feelings are to be traced back to the fact that Central Park represents nature to him, even if it was man-made. To him it is an enhanced form of nature. He enjoys the variety of sites and terrains: hillocks and fields, stony outcrops and jungles of foliage, smooth pastures and crowded networks of caves. True to his self-perception as a "traveller" he likes "wandering back and forth among these different sectors, for it allowed me to imagine I was traveling over great distances, even as I remained within the boundaries of my miniature world" (pp. 68–70).
- Marco enjoys the extraordinary generosity and help of strangers in Central Park which always comes as a great surprise to him, especially as he never asks for anything. In in his continuing self-absorption he devises a philosophical theory to explain this paradox: you get what you want and need most only in a consciousness of not wanting anything. Only then the miracles would happen, "like a bolt from the blue" (p. 66).
- The life down-and-out in the park confronts Marco with various humiliations (e.g. people and children laughing at him, when he searches the garbage for food), but he turns these experiences into a test of character and wards them off with a stiff upper lip.
- The rocks of the park provide protection against the terrible rain and the cave is his last and only retreat in his almost fatal illness.

II,4

Losing Kitty

- His love for Kitty sweeps Marco away and turns him into a new personality. He feels that the conditions of his former life of isolation and fragility, i.e. "his inner walls" (p. 99), are shattered; he compares this experience to the effects of an eartquake.
- In September 1970 Marco and Kitty move to a loft in Chinatown "to set up house together" (p. 224). For the following "eight or nine" months (ibid.) Marco lives in a state of great bliss: his infatuation with Kitty grows, they live a life of great harmony ("supernatural harmony", p. 272), and due to Effing's 'heritage' of 7,000 dollars they do not have to worry about money.
- Kitty pursues her dream of becoming a dancer with great ambition and zeal. She loves attending classes at the world-famous Juilliard School. Her great sense of independence shines through when she insists on additionally taking up the job of a secretary. She does not want to rely on someone else's money.
- All happiness crumbles when Kitty tells Marco that she is pregnant. Although they know they love each other deeply, they quarrel intensively over long periods whether to have an abortion. Both do not budge away from their contrary views. During wild arguments they hurt each other and within a few weeks fatal damage is done to their relationship.
- To Marco becoming a father and therefore being part of a family is an existential event in his life. To him having an abortion is fundamentally wrong. He argues that it would be the same thing as committing murder (p. 273), and: "If you kill our baby, you'll be killing me along with it" (ibid.).
- Marco concedes that all 'the reasons' are on Kitty's side. They are too young to be parents, Kitty would have to give up her dream and her career as a dancer. If we can believe Marco, to Kitty a baby does only exist until it is born (p. 272). She does not seem to question a woman's right to have an abortion.
- After the abortion both draw inwards and "lapse into silence" (p. 274). Marco displays an attitude full of reproach to her ("my whole life had been taken away from me", ibid.), although he knows that in those difficult days he should have comforted Kitty and signaled her his understanding. He is unable to do this and partly out of disgust at his own ugliness and stubborness he feels forced to leave her.
- Some later attempts at reconciliation fail just because of trivial reasons; basically however they fail because of Kitty's clear-sightedness and her feeling that the common ground of their love has been destroyed.

II,5

Female Characters

Flat characters

- Emily Fogg: after her affair she bravely bears the consequences all alone and masters the situation by keeping details and names to herself; she never thought of an abortion.
- Mrs. Hume: the motherly, efficient and good-natured housekeeper; stereotypically equipped with a big bosom.
- Elizabeth Wheeler: a frigid and cold wife; mentally deranged in the end.
- Dora Shamsky: shrewd, quarrelsome, egotistic, addicted to alcohol.
- Mrs. Dunn: warm-hearted and helpful.
- Aunt Clara: lively vaudeville actress enjoying life.

Kitty

- Kitty is characterized in great detail. She is portrayed as the increasingly superior and dominant partner in their relationship. She is reliable and has a firm grasp on the facts of life. She is warm-hearted, open and reserved at the same time. In view of her sensitiveness and empathy towards Marco she surprises the reader with her strong will in the questions of abortion and her career. She also does not waver when Marco tries to win her back.
- Marco as the narrator and master of the narrative material gives only limited prominence to Kitty and their relationship. But he dwells in great detail on her beauty, her artful dancing and her sex appeal.
- Marco's narration representing his service with Effing which expands for almost half a year, only superficially and fleetingly touches on their young love which, as Marco claims. has made a whole world of difference to him. Similarly the narrator later loses track of their story inspite of stating his unique bliss in their common flat. Instead he is preoccupied with his contacts to Sol Barber who at that time is really a stranger to him. Kitty's only appearance for quite some narrative time in this period is as a silent guest at a restaurant dinner with Marco and Sol Barber. On the whole Kitty and the relationship of the young couple do not play an integral part to Marco's view of the past.

II,6

Blakelock: *Moonlight*

- The comparatively small painting (69 cm × 81 cm) presents a calm landscape in the American West.
- In its center there is a full, white moon illuminating the sky, the low mountains on the horizon, and a natural setting with Indians in the foreground.
- The natural terrain is formed by a lake, trees and a brook that divides two small open areas peopled by Indians.
- On the left Marco can discern a small group of Indians sitting at a campfire near a teepee; set a bit apart to the right of a large tree there is the silhouette of a solitary figure on horseback seemingly lost in meditation.
- In the dark and shadowy area of the right bank Marco can only recognize some small trees in a tiny patch of brightness which might be the remnant of another fire.
- The sky with the same color as the earth, the night bright as day, and humans reduced to small silhouettes against the luminous horizon – these aspects are proof to Marco that Blakelock's painting does not strive at realism and to present an actual landscape.
- "The landscape of inwardness and calm" (pp. 158–159) is to represent the idyll of the Indian world in which there still is harmony of man and nature, of heaven and earth. In this American idyll man is at peace with himself and his world.
- Considering the year of origin (1885) Marco presumes that the painting with the Native Americans in a primeval landscape is meant as a document of a lost world.

II,7

The Moon

In Auster's novel the moon is made use of in numerous contexts. The respective meanings differ greatly from each other so that any attempt at reducing the moon to one symbolic meaning – however complex – will fail: "The moon is many things all at once, a touchstone" (Paul Auster, *The Art of Hunger*, New York 1993, p. 315). Some of the "things":

- The idea that nothing is certain, that the course of life is unaccountable and dominated by irrational forces is central to the novel, i.e. central to the narrator's world view. The existence of a rational order which allows man to be master of his life and fate – a view held by Effing – is negated by Marco. To him chance, irrational coincidences indicate that some fickle force like the moon determines man's fate. Uncle Victor's bands who are constantly undergoing some change, pay tribute to the moon in taking her up in their names ("Moonlight Moods", "Moon Men"). Marco's eventful life with sudden turns, ups and downs is accompanied by the moon: The day Marco takes the last of Victor's books to the second-hand store, the astronauts deface the moon and her magical powers; when Marco's journey ends at the Pacific the moon rises as bright and round as in the Blakelock painting.

- The moon as the home of "radiant Diana" (p. 39) stands for the irrational forces in man: love, madness ('lunacy'), illusion, dreams. In contrast to the Barbers the Foggs have an inclination for aimlessness, dreaming and eccentric behavior. When Marco gives a prostitute a lecture on the poems of Sir Walter Raleigh, she calls him "a lunatic" (p. 26). The impression Marco leaves on common people like the caretaker Hernandez, the doctors at his physical and the rabbi at Sol Barber's burial makes them think of lunacy, i.e. mental insanity. In his reaction to Marco's life story the pragmatic and matter-of-fact Effing says: "You're a dreamer, boy. Your mind is on the moon"; and as if to prove this right, Marco out of the blue maintains that he has all prepared to enter upon a career as a librarian: "Libraries aren't in the real world, after all. They're places apart, sanctuaries of pure thought. In that way, I can go on living on the moon for the rest of my life" (p. 214).
- The moon as a celestial body has long evoked man's spirit to venture into the unknown and finally reach the moon by going out into space. Marco is fascinated by Cyrano de Bergerac and his book about his trip to the moon (pp. 45–46; p. 113).
- For a nation whose history is determined by its people always trying to reach new frontiers the moon project of 1969 is of greatest importance as it reaches out for a "frontier" beyond the earth (pp. 39–40).
- The Moon Palace neon sign first seems to signify Uncle Victor's consent to Marco's decision to move into this flat alone, but in his fast changing moods he comes to see the sign as an enigmatic oracle which plunges him into to endless and maddening reflexion. In his hallucinations close to death in Central Park Marco has the vision of the two O's of the word 'moon'. To him they signify the eyes of a scornful God who reproaches him for having gone astray. It is no surprise that Marco with his rich literary knowledge is led to resort to a popular but nevertheless impressive image of American literature in his deepest crisis (Dr. T. Ecklesburg's eyes in *The Great Gatsby* by F. Scott Fitzgerald).
- When on his first evening in Central Park Marco is lost in outer and inner darkness, there are no moon and stars in the sky. The moon as a means to find your direction and your position in nature and life is later affirmed by Thomas Effing: "A man can't know where he is on earth except in relation to the moon or a star." (p. 154)

II,8

Being a traveller

Being on the way to some distant and hardly known territory is one of the novel's main leitmotifs which in many ways is mirrored in the protagonists' courses of life and in many of the literary allusions given in the novel.

- Motivation: inquisitiveness to reach out beyond present boundaries; urge to see if one's conceptions about countries, regions, celestial bodies can be confirmed; fulfilling one's youthful dreams; finding satisfaction in successfully overcoming dangers; mastering extraordinary challenges; seeking to test the limits of one's strength (examples: Saint Brendan, Marco Polo, Columbus, Cabeza de Vaca, Sir Walter Raleigh, Cyrano de Bergerac, Phileas Fogg, Neil Armstrong).
- The journey West: The journey from the overcivilized, urbanized East to the 'wild' West, to frontier areas is a concept deeply rooted in US American cultural and social history. The ideas of a new beginning, of a rebirth, of coming to terms with onself in the vastness of the country and the experience of the awe-inspiring western landscape run deep in the American consciousness of literature, movies and art. The painter J. Barber starts his expedition to the West with the intention to find a new and more genuine approach for his painting. He partly succeeds, but all his pictures are lost. In the end, however, his western adventure makes him a new person equipped with a new identity.
- Marco who at his mother's grave is all of sudden supplied with the missing links of his identity is at the same time robbed of the liefelong picture he has had of himself. To come to terms with his new identity he almost unconsciously sets out for a long, harduous and solitary journey across the West to the Pacific.
- Although Marco's journey in the first part of the novel is confined to Manhattan the various stages and places of his New York itinerary nevertheless shape his experiences in his quest for identity. Stages and places:
  1. protected life in the College dormitory (Columbia University);
  2. the experiment to live an isolated and minimal life in his apartment (West 112th Street);
  3. the retreat to Central Park;
  4. the recovery from self-neglect in Zimmer's apartment (West Village);
  5. the confrontation with his "mentor's" provoking views on art, language, and order of the universe (Th. Effing's huge flat on West Side looking out onto the Hudson);
  6. the initiation into love and sex in a blissful relationship to Kitty (loft in Chinatown).
- All in all Marco's journey or – as he puts it – his "pilgrimage" (p. 58) up and down Manhattan can thus be well regarded as "picaresque" inspite of

its confinement to an urban area (for the term "picaresque" see this study aid, p. 51).

II,9

Missing Fathers – Lost Sons

Julian Barber / Thomas Effing

- Julian Barber's father is a wealthy industrialist, but his son turns out to be a biting critic of the rising American capitalism. In his completely contrary outlook on life Julian Barber has only contempt for him. Julian insists on becoming a painter and has his will. We can conclude that there is no common ground between them and that a father-son relationship does not exist.
- On the eve of his expedition to the West Julian Barber unkowingly fathers a son who for the following thirty years Barber/Effing does not know about. Even when it would have been possible, Effing does not contact his son whom he has never seen.
- In 1947 Effing has coincidentally found out about the existence, the career and the whereabouts of his son. He does not inform his son Solomon Barber that he has survived his western adventure and that he is still around. Effing is intent on not letting his first life, which he regards as totally concluded, intrude into his second.
- Nevertheless he lays down careful instructions how his son Solomon Barber is to be informed about all this after his death. Only then the self-centered Effing thinks that his son is entitled to know about his father: "'Everyone has a right to know about his own past. I can't do much for him, but at least I can do that'" (p. 195).

Solomon Barber

- Solomon Barber, born in 1917, grows up in the belief that his father whom he has never seen died in Utah in 1916/17. In his childhood and youth Solomon suffers from the absence of his father: He admires his paintings on the walls and at the age of seventeen he even writes a novel based on his father's disappearance (*Kepler's Blood*). He has spent the first fifty years of his life with thinking that his father is dead. After Effing's death Solomon Barber receives Marco's letter and Effing's autobiography and is in this way informed about his father's life and his recent death.
- At the age of 29 Professor Solomon Barber unknowingly fathers an illegitimate son with his favorite student Emily Fogg. Emily successfully conceals her whereabouts and her pregnancy from Solomon Barber.

- Barber has since been unaware of the fact that he has a son. His suspicions must have risen when he receives a letter by a certain Mr. Marco Fogg telling him about Effing's double life. When he finally meets Marco Fogg in October 1970 and sees him enter the hotel lobby he immediately knows that this young man must be his son, as "the resemblance to Emily Fogg is too strong. I recognized her the moment you walked into the room" (p. 232). Like Effing Solomon first keeps this news to himself, but not for fear of being left alone but for fear of losing Marco the minute he tells him the truth.

Marco Fogg
- Marco Fogg grows up in the belief that his father died before he was born.
- The absence of his father is painful to him, but especially after his mother's death his Uncle Victor fills in this empty space by providing him with an admirable male role model. It is no wonder then that Uncle Victor's sudden death hits him as hard as if he had lost a father. With his mother's death ten years before he now feels orphaned twice over.
- Solomon Barber withholds his knowledge from his son Marco for more than half a year. When finally Solomon Barber confesses all to Marco Fogg at Emily Fogg's grave, Marco is utterly taken aback. The picture of himself as a lonely orphan dissolves and "the whole world began to rearrange itself" (p. 284) before Marco's eyes. In a first impulse Marco is overwhelmed by anger, nausea and disgust; he rages around screaming like a madman.
- Barber takes a few steps back and then the huge man falls into a freshly dug out grave. With a confused mind Marco spends quite some time at Solomon Barber's hospital bed, only hesitatingly reconciling himself with the fact this enormous man is his father, the father of an extremely lean and haggard son. The difference could not be greater. However, when after long hours at Barber's bedside Marco studies Barber's face he realizes all of sudden that he is looking at himself (p. 289).

II,10

Penance
- As Effing feels that his life approaches its end, he thinks it is time to give some of his material success back to the world. In a mixture both of doing good for past sins and of performing an eccentric, a "lunatic" (p. 207) show on April Fool's Day he and Marco Fogg distribute 400 fifty-dollar notes to anonymous strangers in the streets: "we would perform a series of swift guerilla attacks in a number of carefully selected areas" (p. 202) in

Manhattan. In his fight with the Gresham brothers out there in Utah in 1917 Effing committed murder and came into the possession of unlawful money which he later on redoubled so that he feels now compelled to make good and to pay back "an outstanding debt" (p. 201).

- In California (1917–19) Effing amasses a vast fortune within a short span of time. As his second identity begins to be detected, he withdraws to a life in darkness and immoral pleasures. In a nightly accident he is crippled and is further on confined to a wheelchair. He considers this to be a just punishment. In the spirit of remorse he reconciles himself with the fact that will not be able to walk on foot for the rest of his life and bears this handicap as a kind of plaque of visible penance.
- In his zig-zag quest for identity Marco turns from the "total selfishness" of his nihilistic experiment to "total selflessness" in the days afterwards (p. 80). Towards his friends he confesses repentance for his excesses of self-absorption and for not having turned to them in his crisis: "I wanted to atone for my errors, to make amends to the people who still cared about me […]. I would think of others before I thought of myself" (ibid.).

II,11

Chance and coincidences

There are manifold coincidences sprouting up in all parts of the novel:

- 1492 books – Columbus sets foot on the new world in 1492;
- Armstrong – first man on the moon and the police officer in Boise; while Armstrong makes man's first step on the moon, Marco turns his steps to the bookstore to sell the last of Victor's books;
- the quizzical text of his fortune cookie appears again in Tesla's writings (Tesla the "lunatic", p. 145).

Chance appears as the dominant force in man's fate:

- Marco gets to know Kitty only because they coincidentally wear the same T-shirt.
- He is rescued by chance by Zimmer and Kitty in Central Park.
- Marco applies for a job to assist a handicapped man who turns out to be his grandfather.
- Effing comes to know about the existence of his son Solomon Barber when his companion Pavel Shum by chance brings home a history book written by a certain Solomon Barber.

Chance also withholds desirable occurences:

- The paths of Uncle Victor with Marco and Solomon Barber crossed in 1959, but an actual meeting would not come about: "We were always in the right place at the wrong time, the wrong place at the right time, always just missing each other, always just a few inches from figuring the whole thing out. That's what the story boils down to, I think. A series of lost chances" (p. 245).

- Solomon Barber's scheme to reconcile Kitty with Marco fails, just because she coincidentally catches sight of Marco a second too early.
- The pragmatic Effing ridicules Marco's theories of chance and coincidence; according to him the order of the world bases on laws, e.g. the laws of electricity in which everything is connected to each other. To him the supreme force in ordering one's personal life is pure will power. Man is the master of his destiny and so Effing even masterminds a plan for his own death: "He had announced that May twelfth would be the fatal day" (p. 214), and he does die on that day just two minutes past midnight.

II,12

The end of Marco's journey

- Since the confusing days of finding and soon losing his father again Marco tries to reassert himself as a descendant of Solomon Barber and Thomas Effing. His efforts to win Kitty back fail, so that he again plunges into a haranguing crisis. He takes Barber's car and instinctively turns West to Utah where the hugeness and emptiness of the land supplies him – as it did to his grandfather Effing – with a new perception of the earth and time: He acquires a very detached view of the earth and life on it. He manages to see our planet as the smallest object in the universe (p. 303).
- As the area where his grandfather's cave must have been has vanished by being flooded (Lake Powell) Marco abruptly ends his quest to relive his grandfather's experiences in the West. "I had always known that I would have to stop sooner or later, but I never imagined it happening so abruptly, with such devestating finality" (p. 296).
- Marco's car with all his money (about 12,000 dollars) is stolen and thinking that he is forced to take up the challenge of some malicious god who only seeks to crush him, Marco sets out for an enormous march. For three months he walks on foot through the far West to California. He finds himself heading for the Pacific "borne along by a growing sense of happiness [...]. I had only to keep walking to know that I had left myself behind, that I was no longer the person I had once been" (p. 297).
- The moon that comes up behind the hills of Laguna Beach on January 6th 1972, resembles the moon of Blakelock's painting: full, round and bright hopefully illumating a scene expressing harmony and inner peace.
- The fact that he has come to the end of hier journey on January 6th, the Christian day of epiphany or 'revelation', hints at the significance of this event as a 'personal revelation' for Marco.

III,1

Marco's letter

An appeal or a a final reckoning?

- stating his new won peace of mind, speaking about his more mature insight into the facts of life, apologizing for his stubborness and inflexibility, explaining his intention to start anew, inviting her to come to California to stay in touch;
- criticizing and blaming her for her 'egotism', for giving him up so easily, for being insensitive to his personal problems.

III,2

Marco's aestheticism: life as a work of art

Marco's idea of life as a form of art seems to express the dimension of his personal identity crisis in a very apt way. At present the sequence of events of his life are determined by coincidence, his actions are incoherent and there is no plan or aim – just like a novel without a plot. When after the death of Uncle Victor – his only psychic support – Marco loses his life's foundation, he evades reality and escapes into a philosophical construct of leading a life of nihilism, void of any pragmatic, life-subsisting consideration. This attitude basically resembles the approach of an artist who creates his work of art only along inherent aesthetic principles. By voicing theses ideas Marco acts as Auster´s mouthpiece who in his novels often explores the mutual intrusion of life and art.

IV,1

Explaining Kornblatt's main statements

Effing's role as Marco's spiritual guide, tormentor and benefactor:

- Spiritual guide: With his "assignments" and tasks (e.g. the reading of specific books, exact descriptions of works of art, language use to exactly grasp reality) Effing compels Marco to come to an understanding of relevant sections of the spiritual world of art, philosophy and language (p. 111).
- Tormentor: Facing the absence any forms of politeness or decent behavior in Effing's social manners the sensitive Marco often greatly suffers under this "monster" and "burnt-out maniac" (ibid.). In unfair attacks against his integrity by a malicious Effing, Marco learns to vehemently rebuff and to stand his man in vicious arguments (p. 205).
- Effing in time develops an unusual appreciation of Marco's intelligence and growing robustness against his malicious attacks. In the ludicrous

scenes of giving money away to seemingly deserving strangers they begin to feel that they are kindred spirits.
- Marco becomes impressed by Effing's character as it displays so many facets. He concedes that Effing "had it in him to be a good man" (p. 120). And Effing does good to Marco. He leaves him seven thousand dollars, crumpled bills in a brown paper bag.

Effing's tale
- The reader is both attracted and puzzled when he is confronted by the extremely detailed presentation of a seemingly unconnected life story of an eccentric old man. With Marco getting into contact with Solomon Barber the interrelation of the lives of all three male protagonists is revealed.

The mythology of the American West vs. the gritty New York terrain
- By going back to the lives and art of the painters of the Hudson School of Painting (Thomas Moran, Albert Bierstadt, Ralph Blakelock), who in the second half of the 19th century went on expeditions to frontier areas and Indian territories, the Indian myth of harmony of man and nature can be captured in the novel. When Effing gets lost in the Rocky Mountains he is overwhelmed by their grandness and immense vastness and he undergoes fundamental changes in his outlook on life. He even changes his identity to begin a new life. In stereotypical American fashion this does not happen without murder, robbery and shoot-outs. The frantic San Francisco climate of getting rich fast, of immorality and violence at the beginning of the 20th century is the social and historical background of Effing's rise to wealth and of his loss of physical health.
- To Marco New York stands for overcrowded urbanization and for a life with undue social constraint. Only Central Park offers a refuge. In the novel the late sixties are seen as a time of political turmoil which even seriously endangered the academic life at Columbia University. To Effing New York stands for the addiction to technological progress which with each alleged new step impoverishes man.

IV,2

Kornblatt's main focus

In this passage Kornblatt focuses on how the life of all three male protagonists have been affected by their experiences they make in the American West. The way the West has shaped American identity is reflected in the lives and identities of Effing, Uncle Victor, Marco and even Solomon Barber. They seem to relive stages of American history and the idea of Manifest Destiny on the level of personal history.